Sharpen Your Brain with Bible Puzzles!

Word Searches! • Trivia!
Bible knowledge refreshers!
And more!

Inspired by Faith

Sharpen Your Brain with Bible Puzzles!
ISBN 978-1-7375562-8-2
Published by Product Concept Mfg., Inc.
2175 N. Academy Circle #7, Colorado Springs, CO 80909

©2022 Product Concept Mfg., Inc. All rights reserved.

Written and Compiled by Patricia Mitchell
in association with Product Concept Mfg., Inc.

Scriptures used are from the King James Version of the Bible.

Sayings not having a credit listed are contributed by writers
for Product Concept Mfg., Inc. or in a rare case,
the author is unknown.

Sharpen
Your
Brain
with
Bible
Puzzles!

A wise man will hear,
and will increase learning...

Proverbs 1:5

SHARPEN UP YOUR BIBLE KNOWLEDGE!

These challenging and fun puzzles will not only refresh your memory of the Bible—you might learn some surprising new facts, too! This big, fun variety collection of word search puzzles, crosswords, brain twisters and more will keep you entertained for hours.

Miraculous!

During His earthly ministry, Jesus performed many miracles to show His power over natural forces. In the word search below, nine of these miracles can be found, each one consisting of two intersecting words. Words read left to right; top to bottom. Cover the word box and see how many you can find without peeking!

LAZARUS RAISED

LEPERS HEALED

LAME WALKED

MUTE SPOKE

SEA CALMED

EYES SAW

DEAF HEARD

WATER [changed to] WINE

CROWD FED

```
H E A R D M O R E D O N
Q U N A E B I R K S N I
N L A Z A R U S N A O M
N E A R F A N E C C L E
S H E P H I C A L M E D
N O L B O S Y E W C R O
T H E A L E D M A J O B
A N P L C D E A L O N A
E Y E S R A S E K W O W
T H R A O L A M E A B A
C O S W W E H U D Y E T
O N F E D A N T W I N E
T H E S P O K E C O O R
```

It's in the Good Book

Test your Bible knowledge by marking these familiar sayings True if they are derived from the Bible, and False if not from the Bible.

1. T F God helps those who help themselves.

2. T F A drop in the bucket.

3. T F Silence is golden.

4. T F Pride goes before the fall.

5. T F Tell the truth and shame the devil.

6. T F Fools jump in where angels fear to tread.

7. T F A penny saved is a penny earned.

8. T F By the skin of your teeth.

9. T F Honesty is the best policy.

10. T F Where there's smoke, there's fire.

11. T F Neither a borrower nor a lender be.

12. T F A little bird told me.

Names Of Jesus Word Search

Almighty
Alpha and Omega
Author
Beloved
Carpenter
Christ

Comforter
Creator
Eternal Father
Healer
Holy One
King of Kings

The Life
Messiah
Redeemer
Shepherd
Son Of God
The Word

```
U  Y  H  N  V  E  R  E  D  E  E  M  E  R  I  J
N  Y  V  W  S  C  O  B  H  O  Y  F  E  Y  D  D
H  F  E  S  H  O  Z  A  O  M  L  K  I  H  U  R
Y  K  T  R  C  E  I  W  Q  A  L  O  M  O  E  O
H  E  I  T  G  S  T  H  E  L  I  F  E  L  A  W
C  S  T  N  S  F  D  S  A  M  W  E  A  Y  G  E
T  O  R  E  G  Y  H  N  I  I  A  E  L  O  E  H
D  L  M  B  R  O  Y  F  E  G  H  S  X  N  M  T
E  R  F  F  G  N  F  R  O  H  T  U  A  E  O  K
V  R  P  K  O  M  A  K  G  T  U  B  H  Y  D  S
O  E  O  S  X  R  O  L  I  Y  D  P  F  M  N  O
L  E  N  T  G  T  T  N  F  N  Y  B  I  M  A  N
E  R  V  E  A  U  Y  E  T  A  G  F  M  N  A  O
B  V  W  O  M  E  K  L  R  L  T  S  V  N  H  F
Y  G  T  F  R  D  R  E  H  P  E  H  S  H  P  G
R  V  E  D  U  N  T  C  R  V  R  D  E  S  L  O
N  C  A  R  P  E  N  T  E  R  P  O  M  R  A  D
```

Ties That Bind

Each group of Bible people shares something in common. From the list below, match the names with the ties that bind them!

DISCIPLES   FISHERMEN   KINGS
MISSIONARIES   NOAH'S SONS   PRIESTS
PROPHETS   SIBLINGS   FAMILY MEMBERS

1. SAUL, DAVID, SOLOMON _____

2. PETER, JOHN, JAMES _____

3. DEBORAH, HULDAH, ANNA _____

4. SHEM, HAM, JAPHETH _____

5. AARON, MIRIAM, MOSES _____

6. ELI, AHIMAAZ, MELCHIZEDEK _____

7. NAOMI, RUTH, ORPAH _____

8. ANDREW, SIMON PETER, JOHN _____

9. PAUL, SILAS, BARNABAS _____

Plant a Tree

A grower couldn't decide what kind of tree to plant, so he planted a variety of trees in his orchard! See if you can find these trees mentioned in the Bible.

FIR
OAK
BRAMBLE
ALMOND

CEDAR
ACACIA
APPLE
OLIVE

FIG
PALM
SYCAMORE

```
B  E  A  P  L  A  I  N  E  E  D  S  O
R  A  N  A  L  M  O  N  D  X  O  Y  U
A  C  U  L  A  M  L  C  R  E  N  C  T
M  H  C  M  P  E  I  A  O  M  O  A  K
B  R  O  O  M  T  V  B  A  P  L  M  Y
L  U  A  P  P  L  E  E  C  L  I  O  T
E  R  M  I  E  M  A  O  A  F  I  R  I
M  T  I  S  X  F  L  M  C  I  V  E  M
E  A  O  I  I  N  F  E  I  G  E  A  E
V  M  M  C  E  D  A  R  A  D  D  M  T
```

Bible Scribes

Fit the names of Bible authors in the grid below, crossing off the names as you fit them in. The first name has been added to get you started.

4 letters
AMOS
EZRA
~~JOEL~~
JOHN
LUKE
MARK
PAUL

5 letters
DAVID
JAMES
MICAH
MOSES
NAHUM
PETER

6 letters
DANIEL
ISAIAH
JOSHUA

7 letters
EZEKIEL
SOLOMON

8 letters
HABAKKUK
JEREMIAH

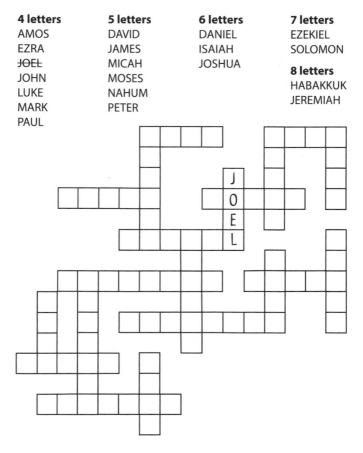

Who's Guilty

Pick the culprit in the lineup!

1. **He led a revolt against Moses.**

   (a) Caleb   (b) Goliath   (c) Korah   (d) Joshua

2. **He wanted to kill David.**

   (a) Saul   (b) Paul   (c) Doeg   (d) Cain

3. **This king of Judah sacrificed his children to idols.**

   (a) David   (b) Ahaz   (c) Ahab   (d) Josiah

4. **His planned massacre was averted.**

   (a) Pashur   (b) Ahab   (c) Joab   (d) Haman

5. **He ordered John the Baptist beheaded.**

   (a) Pilate   (b) Herod

   (c) Annas   (d) Caiaphas

6. **He betrayed His Lord.**

   (a) Judas Priest   (b) Judas Iscariot

   (c) Judas Barsabbas   (d) Judas the brother of James

Look Again!

There are 5 subtle differences between these two pictures. Can you find them?

"I have good news and bad news. The good news is we have enough money for the new church roof. The bad news is... it's still in your pockets."

It All Adds Up!

Find the word each of the three clues have in common. Write it in the blank to the right. These three solutions form a fourth vertical puzzle. The numbers indicate the number of letters in each solution word. The + tells you the word's position.

For example: + **mate**, + **food** and **lost** + is **SOUL**.

+ power   (4)   + _____
+ fully
free +

+ hound   (4)   + _____
+ cast
+ desk

+ time   (5)   + _____
+ shade
+ gown

Final Answer: (4)   _____

                    Hint: God is...

Words of Prayer

God invites us to pray for those who go through struggles, and there are many examples throughout the Bible. Match those who prayed, with the prayer each made to God.

1. Hannah

2. Abraham

3. Paul

4. Moses

5. David

6. Jesus' disciples

7. Solomon

8. Jairus

9. Prodigal son

a. This missionary prayed that God would remove an ailment he called a "thorn in the flesh."

b. He prayed to Jesus that He would restore his little daughter who had died.

c. In the temple, this distraught woman prayed for a baby, and God blessed her with a son, Samuel.

d. He prayed that God would provide a way across the Red Sea and away from pursuing Egyptians.

e. This king prayed for wisdom rather than ask for wealth and glory.

f. He prayed for forgiveness for leaving his father's house and wasting his inheritance.

g. He bargained with God in hopes that enough God-fearing people lived in Sodom to save it.

h. Fearful for their lives, they prayed during a storm on the Sea of Galilee.

i. He prayed for forgiveness for an adulterous relationship and for bringing about a murder.

What Is It?

Test your knowledge by circling the correct definition of these words associated with the Bible:

1. **MITE:**   a. Tree   b. Coin   c. Fish
2. **MANNA:**   a. Desert   b. Bush   c. Food
3. **BAAL:**   a. Altar   b. Idol   c. Haystack
4. **PENTATEUCH:**   a. First five books
   b. Tongues of fire event   c. Satanic symbol
5. **JUDAH:**   a. Holy Land Kingdom
   b. Betrayer of Jesus   c. Branch of the Jordon River
6. **PARABLE:**   a. Song   b. Idea   c. Story
7. **ALMS:**   a. Variety of dates   b. Beasts of burden
   c. Money to the poor
8. **ESCHATOLOGY:**   a. Study of End Times
   b. Doctrine of original sin   c. Study of miracles
9. **EPISTLE:**   a. Weed   b. Female apostle   c. Letter
10. **SABBATH:**   a. Day of rest   b. City of refuge   c. Show of strength
11. **LOGOS:**   a. Toy   b. Word   c. Wood
12. **TIMBREL:**   a. Musical instrument   b. Tableware
    c. Sewing accessory

Hint, Hint...

In this word search, you'll find the highlighted words from the previous page along with their correct definitions.

```
T  R  O  P  L  M  N  U  Y  H  T  A  R  F  E  D
S  T  F  B  R  D  E  W  S  X  A  L  A  A  B  N
T  U  T  J  P  T  B  O  P  L  M  M  U  Y  N  Y
U  B  N  F  M  E  L  M  E  P  I  S  T  L  E  P
D  U  E  I  A  N  N  T  B  R  C  E  W  E  Q  S
Y  L  M  B  N  C  E  T  G  S  D  I  Y  T  T  M
O  Y  U  V  N  W  Q  F  A  M  E  N  Y  T  V  O
F  G  R  W  A  B  U  B  E  T  B  T  R  E  Y  N
E  O  T  W  S  X  B  O  I  R  E  E  M  R  M  E
N  L  S  C  D  A  W  M  I  Y  T  U  T  B  O  Y
D  O  N  I  T  Y  T  B  R  I  V  A  C  P  D  T
T  T  I  H  J  L  P  O  M  N  I  O  S  H  G  O
I  A  L  L  E  R  B  M  I  T  F  E  O  R  N  T
M  H  A  D  U  J  N  O  L  I  M  P  G  O  I  H
E  C  C  H  B  T  C  V  E  O  D  B  O  N  K  E
S  S  I  N  H  U  J  P  A  R  A  B  L  E  D  P
B  E  S  C  F  D  A  Y  O  F  R  E  S  T  N  O
H  B  U  T  G  O  T  W  R  E  D  K  I  M  A  O
L  K  M  H  G  F  O  S  S  Q  W  E  O  T  L  R
E  C  R  D  T  Y  H  D  I  T  M  O  L  L  Y  K
F  I  R  S  T  F  I  V  E  B  O  O  K  S  L  D
V  R  F  B  G  T  M  U  J  Y  N  R  G  B  O  K
O  L  P  K  I  I  D  O  L  B  U  B  Y  Y  H  R
```

Men Of The Bible Word Search

Abel

Noah

Abraham

Job

Moses

Joshua

Samson

Samuel

Saul

David

Elijah

Jonah

Daniel

John The Baptist

Jesus

Peter

Paul

```
Y  G  T  S  I  T  P  A  B  E  H  T  N  H  O  J
R  V  E  D  U  N  T  C  R  V  R  D  E  H  M  I
N  T  F  E  L  T  G  H  J  L  J  O  A  U  I  O
U  Y  J  N  U  E  X  W  D  Y  N  O  L  M  I  J
N  J  O  N  A  H  D  C  U  K  N  H  S  G  Y  N
H  F  B  S  P  X  Z  P  O  M  L  K  I  H  U  N
Y  B  T  V  C  E  S  W  O  A  L  O  M  I  U  H
H  B  Y  T  S  A  M  S  O  N  L  C  I  M  O  A
L  J  J  H  G  F  E  S  A  E  W  E  R  T  V  J
E  C  E  D  T  S  H  N  U  J  M  O  L  M  I  I
P  L  O  S  G  T  Y  M  E  C  W  S  X  C  E  L
V  L  F  B  U  M  A  H  A  R  B  A  G  R  I  E
O  U  P  K  I  S  Y  N  G  B  U  B  E  Y  V  R
D  A  V  I  D  A  D  F  A  K  E  T  F  M  I  P
F  S  N  U  G  T  D  A  N  I  E  L  I  M  O  L
Y  R  V  E  O  U  Y  N  T  P  A  F  M  N  V  C
D  V  W  O  M  I  K  L  P  L  T  G  V  N  B  H
```

Picture the Words!

Can you discover what Bible concept each word-picture suggests?

1.

2.

FA🚶ITH

3.

PASS

4.

GATE

Bible Timeline

Put these events in order as they took place in Bible history:

____ Solomon's Temple is built

____ John the Baptist is born

____ Noah builds an Ark

____ Jesus dies on Calvary and rises on the third day

____ Abraham goes to the Promised Land

____ The Apostle John receives visions of End Times

____ Paul spreads the Gospel during wide-ranging missionary trips

____ Joseph is taken to Egypt

____ King David rules in Jerusalem

____ Gabriel brings a message to Mary

____ God places Adam and Eve in the Garden of Eden

____ Jesus teaches throughout Galilee and Judea

____ Ten Commandments are given to Moses on Mount Sinai

____ Jesus is baptized

Hidden Disciples

The names of seven of Jesus' disciples are hidden in the sentences below. Can you spot them?

I can't stop for this, I'm on a schedule!

_____

If you get in a jam, escape to Philippi!

_____

Matt hewed the tree with one blow of his ax.

_____

For a pet, Erica chose a calico cat.

_____

Be kind and rewind.

_____

Johnnycakes are her specialty.

_____

God's Promise –
When You Need Direction

Cross out one letter of each pair to reveal God's promise to you in the book of Proverbs, chapter 3. Then fill in the verse number.

IT HN   EA CL AL   GT OH DY   SW MA OY AS   LA

BC KI BN LO EW LE   EY ID SG WE   OH IW MO,

RA DN AD   NH DE   GS OH SA PL LE   LD AI MR

FE EC TP TA OH LY   JP EA ST HU ES.

Write your answer below.

_____ .

_____

*Proverbs 3:*_____

Bible Match Ups

Match the name in the first column with the right name in the second column!

Couples

1. Zacharias
2. Hosea
3. Herod
4. Aquila
5. Boaz
6. Zebedee
7. Ananias

a. Herodias
b. Ruth
c. Salome
d. Elizabeth
e. Sapphira
f. Priscilla
g. Gomer

Mothers and Sons

1. Bathsheba
2. Rachel
3. Mary
4. Eunice
5. Hannah
6. Elizabeth
7. Rebekah

a. Jesus
b. John the Baptist
c. Solomon
d. Samuel
e. Jacob
f. Timothy
g. Joseph

What Do You Know About the Bible?

Pick the correct answer from the choices given!

1. The first five books of the Bible:
   a. Gospels   b. Pentateuch   c. Epistles

2. The first four books of the New Testament:
   a. Gospels   b. Pentateuch   c. Epistles

3. The Lord's Prayer can be found in:
   a. Exodus   b. Matthew   c. Corinthians

4. The 10 Commandments can be found in:
   a. Genesis   b. Exodus   c. Haggai

5. The relationship of God to His people is described as:
   a. Zookeeper to animals   b. Weaver to cloth
   c. Shepherd to sheep

6. The Garden of Eden is introduced in:
   a. Genesis   b. Luke   c. Acts

7. Not a parable of Jesus:

a. Prodigal Son   b. Good Samaritan

c. Hare and the Tortoise

8. The last book of the Bible is:

a. Malachi   b. Revelation   c. Thessalonians

9. Not a book in the New Testament:

a. Malachi   b. Revelation   c. Thessalonians

10. Epistle means:

a. History   b. Letter   c. E-document

11. "The Prayer Book of the Bible" is:

a. Genesis   b. Corinthians   c. Psalms

12. The "Great Love Chapter" of the Bible is found in:

a. Genesis   b. Corinthians   c. Psalms

God's Promise –
When You Wonder Where
He Is

Cross out words according to the instructions to reveal a Bible truth.

BREAD   DOVE   LO   ANTS   CORN   I   JOB   AM   EARTH

OWLS   AWAY   FLOUR   LUKE   CAMEL   WITH   OLIVES

YOU   SERPENT   IN   HEAVEN   RUTH   FRUIT   A   ALWAYS

FIGS   MANGER   NUMBERS

Cross out...

1. all books of the Bible.
2. words that form the title of a well-known Christmas carol.
3. the two things God created in the beginning.
4. food items
5. animals

Answer:

_____

Name Above All Names

Unscramble the words to form names for Jesus Christ found in the Bible.

1. S H A S I E M

   _ _ _ _ _ _ _

2. R A Z E A N N E

   _ _ _ _ _ _ _ _

3. E E E E R M R D

   _ _ _ _ _ _ _ _

4. R A M O D I E T

   _ _ _ _ _ _ _ _

5. S E R O C O N U L

   _ _ _ _ _ _ _ _ _

6. L A P A H

   _ _ _ _ _

7. A M E N L U M E

   _ _ _ _ _ _ _ _

Women of the Bible

Choose the correct woman's name for each of these descriptions.

1. She heard God's first promise of a Savior.
   a. Eve
   b. Mary
   c. Martha

2. She gave thanks upon seeing the baby Jesus.
   a. Elizabeth
   b. Miriam
   c. Anna

3. Peter raised her from the dead.
   a. Judith
   b. Anna
   c. Tabitha

4. She had 12 brothers.
   a. Deborah
   b. Dinah
   c. Dorcas

5. She remained faithful to her mother-in-law, Naomi.
   a. Orpah
   b. Ruth
   c. Tamar

6. She was a prophetess consulted by priests and elders.
   a. Huldah
   b. Hannah
   c. Heidi

7. Jesus appeared to her after His resurrection.
   a. Salome
   b. Joanne
   c. Mary Magdalene

Bible Vocabulary

How well do you know the meaning of words that appear in the Bible? Test yourself by circling the best definition!

1. COMMANDMENT
   a. advice
   b. law
   c. suggestion

2. EBENEZER
   a. The Lord has helped us
   b. God is merciful
   c. He has redeemed His people

3. CHRIST
   a. Teacher
   b. Rabbi
   c. Messiah

4. SILOAM
   a. Sent
   b. Peace
   c. Health

5. SABBATH
   a. Day of punishment
   b. Day of birth
   c. Day of rest

6. COMFORTER
   a. Jesus Christ
   b. Holy Spirit
   c. God Almighty

7. JUSTIFIED
   a. Punished by God
   b. Brought near God
   c. Made right with God

8. EPISTLE
   a. Bramble
   b. Letter
   c. Wife of an apostle

All About God Crossword

ACROSS

1 Shows mercy

4 Consoles

7 Not wicked

9 Loyal

10 Restores

11 Delivers

13 Old Testament name

15 Immutable

19 Here now

20 Always was, always will be

22 Maker

23 All-knowing

24 Listens

26 Without error

27 Fair

28 Makes known

DOWN

1 One person of Godhead

2 Second person of Godhead

3 God is ___

5 Three-in-one

6 Mighty

8 His kingdom

12 Compassionate

14 Third person of Godhead

(2 words)

16 Confers happiness

17 Not of earth

18 Instructs

19 Vows

21 Gives this to us

25 Observes

Look Again!

There are 5 subtle differences between these two pictures. Can you find them?

"You can tell the regular churchgoers because if they're missing a spoon, salad bowl, or casserole dish, the first place they look is in the church kitchen."

Ridin' Along

In the list below, find the right vehicle for each rider.

LADDER	CHARIOT	ARK	HORSE
CAMEL	FISH	BOAT	COLT

1. Noah weathered a storm in one.

   _____

2. Jesus entered Jerusalem on one.

   _____

3. The Ethiopian invited Philip to hop right in.

   _____

4. Peter stepped out of his, then wished he hadn't.

   _____

5. Jonah was an unwilling passenger in one.

   _____

6. Jacob saw angels using one in a dream.

   _____

7. Rebekah rode one on her way to meet Isaac.

   _____

8. A rider rode a white one in the book of Revelation.

   _____

Who's Older?

Put these Bible names in order of when they were born, from earliest to latest. The first one has been done for you.

A. _3_ Esther
    _5_ Dorcas
    _1_ Eve
    _4_ Mary
        Magdalene
    _2_ Hannah

B. __ Paul
    __ Jacob
    __ Abel
    __ Matthew
    __ Noah

C. __ King Herod
    __ Timothy
    __ Jesus
    __ Amos
    __ Lot

D. __ Luke
    __ David
    __ Joshua
    __ Micah
    __ Solomon

Prophets Of The Bible Word Search

Amos Hosea Micah
Daniel Isaiah Nahum
Elijah Jeremiah Obadiah
Ezekiel Joel Samuel
Habakkuk Jonah Zephaniah
Haggai Malachi

```
E C Z E P H A N I A H O L M I K
P L O B G T Y H A C I M X C E D
V R L B G T M U J Y N T G B H K
O J E R E M I A H E U B H Y I R
P O I S X A D F Z K L P F M S P
F E N U G T W E O U Y I I M A L
Y L A M O S K N T H A F J N I C
D V D O M I K L P A R G O A A H
U Y H N E E X M D B N N N M H J
N Y V L S I A G G A H H A G Y N
S A M U E L Z P O K L K H H U N
Y B T V A E S W Q K L O M I U U
H B Y C G V T F R U D C I M O M
L K H H G F D S A K W E R T V R
Y I T F R D O B A D I A H H I Y
R V H O S E A C R V R D E S M I
N T F E Y T G H J L P O M U I O
```

Book List

See how well you know your Bible stats! Pick the right answer for each question.

1. What is the longest book of the Bible? (Hint: It has 150 chapters!)
   a. Psalms b. Proverbs c. Revelation

2. How many Gospels are there in the New Testament?
   a. Four b. Six c. Eight

3. How many books are in the KJV Bible?
   a. 64 b. 66 c. 68

4. Who's the oldest person mentioned in the Bible?
   a. Melchizedek b. Malachi c. Methuselah

5. Which is the shortest of these books of the bible?
   a. Philemon b. 2 John c. Jude

6. Who in the Bible traveled the most extensively?
   a. Abraham b. Paul c. Jesus

7. Who's the person, other than Jesus, mentioned the most number of times in the Bible?
   a. Adam b. Moses c. David

Pyramid Play

Help the Children of Israel build Pharaoh's pyramid by thinking of words of increasing length using the letters provided.

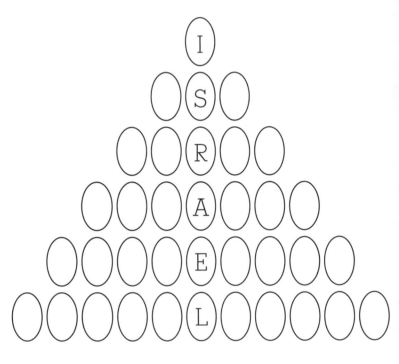

Jacob's Kids

Jacob's 12 sons* and one daughter are missing. Can you find them? Here's the challenge: their names appear right to left; left to right; top to bottom; bottom to top; and on the diagonal!
*These became the twelve tribes of Israel.

```
H A P P Y Z O O F S I M E O N
P I D R O E N L A I S R S P E
E M R E U B E N N S A O T I L
S Y U T W U R Y D S A M H E L
O L E V E L I L T A S H E R I
J U D A H U L E O M N A R U E
U L E L I N E V A L I N T G O
D L N E D T M I S S A C H A R
Y A Y I M Y S O Z Z R A E D Y
O S N A P H T A L I S L L E A
P A U L N I A N H O J E L L E
H M N E Z N N N I M A J N E B
```

Hint: Genesis 35:23-26; 30:21

41

Bible Animals Crossword

ACROSS

2 The devil is like a roaring one

4 Plague hoppers

6 We're like them

10 They will be separated from 6 Across

11 Noah sent one out of the ark

12 Honey providers

14 "Go to the __, thou sluggard" (Prov. 6:6)

15 Big sea creature

18 Sacrificial animal

20 Symbol for the Holy Spirit

22 Associated with Peter's denial

23 Jesus compared King Herod to one (Luke 13:32)

DOWN

1 What Peter wanted to catch

2 Plague pests

3 John the Baptizer's chosen foods

5 Not one falls without God's knowledge

6 Eden tempter

7 The prodigal son fed them

8 Manna supplement

9 Jesus rode into Jerusalem on one

13 Riches "fly away as an ___ toward heaven" (Prov. 23:5)

16 Apocalypse gallopers

17 It ate Jonah's shade plant

19 John the Baptizer wore the hair of one

21 Jesus compares a false prophet to one

43

Bible Places

Can you name these Bible places? Watch out—some are harder than others!

1. Where the walls came tumbling down.

   _____

2. Where the languages were confused.

   _____

3. Jesus spent His boyhood here.

   _____

4. Paul was born here.

   _____

5. John Mark left Paul and went home from here.

   _____

6. Ruth came from here.

   _____

7. After the Resurrection, some disciples decided to walk here.

   _____

8. King David ruled from this city.

   _____

9. Jonah hoped God would destroy this city.

   _____

10. Cain built this city.

    _____

Good Food, Let's Eat!

Choose the correct answer–and bon appetit!

1. Jesus compared the kingdom of heaven to this seed.
   a) Poppy b) Mustard c) Coriander d) Flower

2. Ruth gleaned the fields of Boaz during these harvests.
   a) Corn and maize b) Cocoa and coffee
   c) Soybeans and wheat d) Wheat and barley

3. Jesus saw Nathanael under a tree that bears these.
   a) Figs b) Olives c) Apples d) Dates

4. John the Baptist made these a staple of his diet.
   a) Wasps b) Katydids c) Scorpions d) Locusts

5. At the Last Supper, Jesus blessed these.
   a) Bread and wine b) Milk and honey
   c) Barley cakes and water d) Apples and oranges

6. Jesus fed a multitude of more than 5000 with these.
   a) 7 loaves and 3 fish b) 5 loaves and 2 fish
   c) 2 loaves and 7 fish d) 12 loaves and 1 fish

Bible Men Crossword

ACROSS

2 One of 12 brothers

4 Wicked king of the Old Testament

6 He "walked with God" (Gen. 5:22)

7 1 Down brother

8 NT physician

11 Betrayer

14 God changed his name to Israel

16 Companion of 24 Across

17 Judge at Jesus' trial

19 Patriarch

20 24 Across brother

23 Epistle writer

24 Commandment receiver

25 Ark builder

26 NT king

27 OT king

28 Savior

DOWN

1 5 Down son

2 Gospel writer

3 Israel's first king

5 First man

6 Prophet pursued by 4 Across

9 Tax collector turned disciple

10 Believing Pharisee

12 Went to Tarsus to look for Paul

13 Fisherman turned disciple

15 Eunice's missionary son

18 Raised from the dead

21 19 Across son

22 A fish swallowed him

By the Book

Fourteen books of the Bible are hidden in this paragraph. Can you find them all? Underline your answers.

He who judges, the Bible says, will be himself judged, so the ruthless man repented of his evil acts. "Just look at the numbers!" he remarked in loud lamentations when he realized what a jam, estranged from God, he was in. "This is a revelation to me, and now I want to do a better job." He regrets he was lacking so much in wisdom, and now the man sings praises, psalms, and follows wise proverbs. He is not lukewarm, but firmly believes there is forgiveness in Jesus.

Nine-Patch Puzzler

Rearrange the squares to spell the name of a Bible man or woman. The first one has been done for you.

1.
N	U	C
I	R	S
E	O	L

Cornelius

4.
S	A	M
EL	H	E
H	T	U

_____

7.
E	R	A
S	S	U
H	U	A

_____

2.
H	A	H
P	A	N
I	Z	E

_____

5.
H	A	H
B	A	B
E	T	S

_____

8.
E	E	E
L	C	L
H	I	M

_____

3.
X	D	L
A	N	A
E	R	E

_____

6.
TI	A	U
M	A	S
R	B	E

_____

49

God's Promises –
When You Lack Confidence

Cross out the words according to instructions given to reveal God's promise:

BE NINE HE I SILENT CAN LEFT HEAVEN DO END

HERB FISH ALL HIS MOON ONE THINGS THOU

THROUGH THREE SUN HIM EARTH CHRIST

CREATURES TEN LIGHTS WHICH TIMES WATERS

MY STRENGTHENETH BEHIND GRASS ME STARS

NIGHT VISION.

1. Cross out masculine pronouns.
2. Cross out the name of a popular book series.
3. Cross out the subject of #2.
4. Cross out the name of a familiar hymn.
5. Cross out the name of a Christmas carol.
6. Cross out all numbers.
7. Cross out things mentioned in Genesis 1.

Words to Keep Close in Heart

Using the clues, locate each letter and put it on the line numbered as its clue. The result are words worth remembering.

```
A L M P S H O
E S I K O T Y
O N R S C G U
K A T O J E E
Q E G B A O I
N I C H D P T
U W E R O M L
```

1. This letter is in between a T and E.
2. This letter appears more often than any other letter.
3. This letter is in the sixth row, but no place else on the grid.
4. This letter is in the second and third columns.
5. This letter appears in row one.
6. This letter follows an O and M.
7. This letter is the same as the letter for clue 2.
8. This letter isn't on the grid.
9. This letter is one of the vowels in the last column.

$\overline{}$ $\overline{}$ $\overline{}$ $\overline{}$ $\overline{}$ $\overline{}$ $\overline{}$ $\overline{}$ $\overline{}$
 1   2   3   4   5   6   7   8   9

Look Again!

There are 5 subtle differences between these two pictures. Can you find them?

...the greatest of these is love.

Bible Places Crossword

ACROSS

3 Where God sent Jonah

5 Fire and brimstone city

8 Jesus raised a widow's son here

10 Southern Kingdom

11 Site of Jesus' first miracle

12 Place where Paul lived under house arrest

13 Where Paul preached in the agora

16 Road to ___, where Jesus appeared after His resurrection

20 Its walls came tumbling down

21 Witch of ___

23 Plagues place

24 Tower of ___

26 Where Jesus healed the possessed man

DOWN

1 Jesus' birthplace

2 Dorcas' home

4 Where Jesus grew up

6 Mount of ___

7 City associated with Paul's conversion

9 Site of Jesus' crucifixion

10 Temple site

14 City of early Christian congregation

15 Garden where Jesus prayed

17 Ten Commandments mount

18 Mary and Martha's home

19 Abraham's birthplace

22 Land of milk and honey

25 First garden

Kids in the Bible

Kids play an important part in the history of God's people!
Match the child with the event in which he or she played a part.

1. Boy with 5 loaves and 2 fish

2. A prostitute's infant

3. Jairus' daughter

4. Rhoda

5. Moses

6. Jesus

7. Nobleman's son

8. Samuel

9. Isaac

a. Raised from the dead by Jesus

b. Adopted by Pharaoh's daughter

c. Healed by Jesus from a distance

d. Entered temple service as a child

e. Feeding of the 5,000

f. Servant girl

g. Case showing Solomon's wisdom

h. Abraham's long-awaited son

i. Sat among scholars in the temple

Women Of The Bible Word Search

Mary	Anna	Martha	Huldah
Ruth	Dorcas	Miriam	Rachel
Hannah	Elizabeth	Judith	Naomi
Esther	Mary Magdalene	Tabitha	Priscilla
Deborah	Gomer	Dinah	Rebekah
Eve	Joanna	Orpah	
Sarah	Leah	Tamar	

```
O  L  H  A  N  N  A  H  G  B  U  B  H  Y  V  R
P  E  W  S  X  A  D  F  H  N  A  O  M  I  F  A
F  R  U  T  H  T  W  N  U  U  Y  B  I  M  O  L
E  V  E  A  A  U  Y  N  L  X  R  A  C  H  E  L
D  V  N  O  P  I  K  L  D  T  T  G  V  N  L  I
Y  I  T  M  R  D  E  S  A  A  Q  A  E  E  I  C
D  V  E  A  O  N  T  B  H  T  R  L  E  S  Z  S
N  T  F  R  Y  T  I  H  J  L  A  O  M  T  A  I
U  Y  C  T  V  T  X  A  D  D  N  M  M  H  B  R
N  A  V  H  H  E  H  R  G  E  O  H  A  E  E  P
S  N  E  A  Q  T  Z  A  G  B  L  K  I  R  T  N
Y  N  T  V  I  E  M  S  Q  O  L  O  R  I  H  U
H  A  Y  T  G  Y  T  H  R  R  M  C  I  M  O  M
L  O  J  H  R  F  A  N  N  A  W  E  M  T  V  A
E  J  R  A  T  E  H  N  I  H  M  O  R  M  I  R
P  L  M  B  L  T  R  E  B  E  K  A  H  C  E  Y
V  R  J  U  D  I  T  H  J  Y  N  T  G  B  I  K
```

Relationships

Bible people had relatives—some of whom they got along with, others they didn't. Determine the relationships between these Bible pairs.

1. Moses was to Jethro as Ruth was to:
   a. Zipporah   b. Orpah   c. Naomi   d. Mary

2. Leah was to Rachel as Martha was to:
   a. Mary   b. Esther   c. Sarah   d. Joanna

3. Potiphar was to Joseph as Philemon was to:
   a. Pharaoh   b. Onesimus   c. David   d. Silas

4. Timothy was to Lois as Jacob was to:
   a. Isaac   b. Esau   c. Nahor   d. Abraham

5. Lazarus was to Mary as Aaron was to:
   a. Sarah   b. Miriam   c. Dorcas   d. Deborah

6. Abraham was to Sarah as David was to:
   a. Jesse   b. Tamar   c. Michal   d. Mary

7. Priscilla was to Aquila as Rebekah was to:
   a. Isaac   b. Jacob   c. Abraham   d. Joseph

Day Job

Match the Bible name with his or her line of work!

Deborah   a. Shepherd

Paul   b. Tax Collector

Baruch   c. Fisher

Luke   d. Judge

Zacchaeus   e. Tailor

Lydia   f. Tentmaker

Andrew   g. Merchant

Amos   h. Scribe

Dorcas   i. Physician

Shared Letter

In each line of four Biblical names, there's one shared letter between all four names. Put the shared letter from each line on the blanks below to form another Biblical name.

1. Absalom   Elisha   Saul   Esther

2. David   Adam   Malachi   Mary

3. Moses   Samson   Naomi   Martha

4. Jesus   Jairus   Paul   Uriah

5. Gideon   Gomer   Herodias   Hezekiah

6. Jezebel   Israel   Silas   Elijah

Answer:

___ ___ ___ ___ ___ ___
 1   2   3   4   5   6

Alpha and Omega

These Bible-connected words begin and end with the same letter. Use a different letter for each word.

Example: __ NN __ Anna

1. __ EN __

2. __ BB __

3. __ EA __

4. __ IRIA __

5. __ AI __

6. __ AVI __

7. __ AGL __

8. __ CACI __

9. __ IDO __

10. __ ULE __

11. __ EE __

12. __ IVE __

Bible Women Crossword

ACROSS

1 Early Christian teacher

5 Driven into the desert
  by 13 Across

6 Bore John, who became
  a Baptizer

10 Timothy's pious
  grandmother

13 Her name means "Princess"

15 First woman

17 Jacob's favored wife

19 She learned the secret
  of Samson's strength

20 Samuel's mom

23 Nabal's smart wife

24 Desert prophetess

DOWN

2 She stayed with 21 Down

3 Temple widow

4 Early Christian known
  for her needlework

7 Seller of purple cloth

8 Timothy's pious mother

9 Hosea's unfaithful wife

11 Solomon's mom

12 Sister of Lazarus

14 Wicked queen

16 Queen of Persia

18 She had 12 brothers

21 Orpah's mother-in-law

22 Magdalene

Look Again!

There are 5 subtle differences between these two pictures. Can you find them?

"Mom, I can't believe you really dressed that way when you were my age!"

Notable Events

Test your knowledge of Christian history by picking the correct definition of each:

1. The Crusades

a. Attempted conquest of the Holy Land during the 11th century.

b. Tent revival meetings throughout the U.S.

c. A series of best-selling Christian adventure stories.

2. The Diet of Worms

a. Title of a cookbook for unrepentant sinners.

b. Contentious religious debates of the 21st century.

c. Assembly in which Martin Luther was asked to recant his works.

3. The Sunday School Movement

a. Initially established to teach illiterate adults and children to read and write.

b. Initially established as a place to park the kids while parents went out for breakfast.

c. Initially established to supplement a church service.

4. Tyndale's Bible

a. First Latin Bible published.

b. First English Bible published.

c. First Gaelic Bible published.

5. The Jesus Movement

a. Crowds who followed Jesus during His ministry on earth.

b. All who believe the Good News of Jesus Christ.

c. Antiestablishment Christianity of the 1960s.

6. The Temperance Movement

a. Anti-alcohol.

b. Anti-anger.

c. Pro moderate temperatures.

Letter Mix

Cross out each letter from the alphabet list that you see in the box below. Rearrange the letters remaining in the alphabet list to form the name of one of Jesus' disciples.

A B C D E F G H I J K L M N O P Q R S T U V W X Y Z

C	V	S	H	L	P	G
B	U	I	Z	J	F	O
C	Q	G	V	Y	M	O
H	K	T	I	L	Q	U
K	X	Z	Y	S	M	Z
C	H	Q	K	O	U	P
S	Y	M	S	L	F	B
H	X	V	Z	K	M	C
I	P	I	F	G	L	Y
X	H	S	P	T		

Answer: _____

Look Again!

There are 5 subtle differences between these two pictures. Can you find them?

On the road of life, good friends are God's way
of keeping us on the right path.

God's Promise –
When You're in Need

Find God's promise hidden in these words by following the instructions below:

1. Cross out all books of the Bible.
2. Cross out the name of a familiar hymn.
3. Cross out a saying by Benjamin Franklin.
4. Cross out the name of a biblical garden.
5. Cross out the names of various foods and herbs.

A LEAD PENNY ASK NUTS AND JONAH THOU SAVED

HOSEA YE ME IS BARLEY SHALL A RECEIVE FIGS

ON THAT EDEN BREAD PENNY ONIONS JOB YOUR

AMOS EGGS EARNED JOY MAY BE SALT MINT JOEL

BEANS FULL FISH.

Bible verse: _____

_____

_____

Picture the Words!

Can you discover what Bible concept each word-picture suggests?

1. JACOB JACOB JACOB JACOB

2. DO EVERYTHING

3. Hitrustm

4. + 🎀

Words of a Feather

In each word-block below, there are three associated words, such as: **APPLE, PEAR, APRICOT.** Cross out the associated words. Write the first letter of each remaining word on the blanks below to spell out what Samuel said in answer to God's call.

SERMON SHEEP PATIENCE HYMN EWE ANNA KEEP
PEW FULLNESS OMRI

REIGN THANK KING HONEST YEAST SAVE CROWN
EZRA RACHEL THRONE

VINE LOVE ADORE NEEDS TEKOA JOY HALLELUJAH
PEACE ESAU ABEL

WORDS RAMAH DEEDS EDOM TRINITY HOLY
THOUGHTS

Bible verse: ____ ____ ____ ____ ____ ____ ____ ____

____ ____ ____ ____ ____ ____ ____ ____ ____ ____

____ ____ ____ ____ ____ ____ ____ .

Choices

Find answers by choosing one letter from each pair of letters, reading left to right.

Example: Eden was one
IG   EA   RC   ED   ET   ON

1. A candle should not be covered with one
   BC   EU   VS   OH   EI   LM

2. Bible bread ingredient
   WB   AH   RA   LE   TE   TY

3. Ark measures
   MC   UI   LB   IS   GT   MS

4. Moses parted it
   RM   EA   OD   ST   OE   AY

5. Jesus rode one into Jerusalem
   SD   OE   NJ   EK   EI   YN

6. House of worship
   CT   AH   UA   OR   CV   EH

7. Day of worship for many
   TS   EU   ND   ED   IA   YN

Names of Jesus Crossword

The Bible and Christians refer to Jesus in many ways. Solve the clues below to fill in the crossword.

ACROSS

2 Prince of ___

5 Bread of ___

6 ___ and Omega

(Rev. 1:8)

7 Messiah

11 ___ of Bethlehem

12 ___ of the World

15 "God with us"

16 ___ of David

17 Physician

18 ___ Child

20 Good ___

DOWN

1 ___ from on high

(Luke 1:78)

3 Rabbi

4 Jesus ___

8 One who saves

9 "God of Israel"

10 Jesus of ___

12 The Word

13 "I am the way, the ___"

(John 14:6)

14 ___ worker

19 ___ of God

Missing Pages

Every other letter has been omitted from these Books of the Bible. How quickly can you fill in the blanks?

__ A __ G __ I

__ H __ L __ M __ N

__ A __ A __ I __ N __

__ B __ D __ A __

__ C __ L __ S __ A __ T __ S

__ E __ R __ W __

__ H __ L __ P __ I __ N __

__ A __ A __ K __ K

__ A __ U __

__ S __ L __ S

__ I __ O __ H __

__ O __ O __ S __ A __ S

Double Trouble Word Search

There are 23 Bible-related words, each containing a set of double letters. The first one is done for you.

Aaron	Fulfillment	Isaac	Sheep
Accusers	Good	Keep	Struggle
Beersheba	Greed	Look	Suffer
Colossians	Habakkuk	Matthew	Philippians
Deed	Haggai	See	Weep
Ecclesiastes	Heed	~~Seek~~	

```
O O W L S O M E U M E L O O K S A W
I S E E K S A A R O N E N S U I G E
B R E E A S T C A O R N B E A D R S
C E P J T O T C L H A G G A I I E S
A A S P E N H E E D B E O O D E E D
V R A Y M T E Q U E S M P O R T D O
R A C L A I W R E S S O M M D R I M
E C C L E S I A S T E S E E T T L E
J E U V E A X T C O L O S S I A N S
S U S S E A I A R R N O T R P R I H
E T E R C C O H A B A K K U K E O E
S T R O O P B E E R S H E B A A N E
R E S U F F E R I C C A E P R M I P
P L U G G E P H I L I P P I A N S O
A I L A A G E W C O Z Z I L L E E D
F U L F I L L M E N T E P L L E E V
I U A F H E L E W E O D P A O T L O
```

Look Again!

There are 5 subtle differences between these two pictures. Can you find them?

"I've been thinking a lot about the hereafter, Pastor...More and more often, I find myself standing in a room thinking 'Now what did I come in hereafter?'"

Let's Eat!

In the puzzle, circle the Bible foods listed in the word box. Words may read forward, backward, up, down, or diagonally. The letters remaining, in order, spell part of a common table prayer!

ANISE	CORN
MINT	FISH
SALT	WHEAT
BEANS	HONEY
BARLEY	EGGS
MUSTARD	MILK
LEEKS	WINE
FIGS	LAMB
NUTS	RUE
OLIVES	RYE

```
E N I W F L A M B
L S E V I L O E D
T A T H S E S R M
L E N G H I A F I
E R M I N T T S L
E U T O S U B S K
K E B U B E A N S
S E M E N B R Y E
L G E S U T L A S
S G I E T A E H W
D S A F S M Y E N
C O R N Y E N O H
```

Answer:

_____

_____

_____

_____

_____

Church Meeting

Enter the names of everyone who attended the church meeting. The first name has been entered for you. (Anyone think to ask the Lord to come?)

3 Letters	4 Letters	5 Letters
Asa	Abel	Aaron
Dan	Adam	Abram
~~Eve~~	Amos	David
Ham	Anna	Hosea
Job	Cain	Jacob
	Esau	James
	John	Jesse
	Levi	Moses
	Lois	Peter
	Luke	Rhoda
	Mark	Rufus
	Noah	Simon

83

Look Again!

There are 5 subtle differences between these two pictures. Can you find them?

O Come Let Us Adore Him

Parables Of Jesus Word Search

Lamp Under A Basket
The Sower
The Weeds
Mustard Seed
Hidden Treasure
Lost Sheep

Wedding Feast
Fig Tree
Good Samaritan
Wise Man's Foundation
Prodigal Son
Rich Man And Lazarus

```
L W E D D I N G F E A S T M I T
N W E W S E D C U K O H H G E N
H I E S Q X E P O M L K E K U N
Y S D E E W E H T A L O S I N S
H E Y T G V R F R E D A O M O U
L M J H G F T S A Q B E W T V R
E A U D T Y G N I A M O E M I A
P N O S G T I F R C W S R C E Z
V S F B T T F E J Y N T G B I A
O F P K I A D P E E H S T S O L
P O W S X N R F A K D P F M N D
F U N U U T W D O U Y B I M O N
Y N V P O U Y N S X A F M N S A
D D M O M I K L P E T G V N L N
Y A T F R D E S W A E A M H A A
L T E D U N T C R V R D E I G M
N I E R U S A E R T N E D D I H
G O O D S A M A R I T A N B D C
O N P K I M Y N G B U B H Y O I
W E W S X A D F A K D P F M R R
F E N U G T W N O U Y B I M P L
```

God's Promise When You Pray

Follow the directions to reveal God's promise to you when you pray to Him.

1. In even-numbered lines, cross out books of the Bible.
2. In line 3, cross out two repeated words.
3. In odd-numbered lines, cross out rhyming words.
4. Cross out the name of a Christmas carol hidden in one of the lines.
5. In lines 2 and 3, cross out words related to gardening.
6. In line 1, cross out words ending in d.
7. In line 5, cross out words ending in l.
8. In lines 1, 4 and 5, cross out desk items.

1. the ruler Lord eyes land night pen of the lifted light lied
2. plant acts Lord reap are kings flower upon hoe judges the
3. soil the righteous seed star sow and his plant the far fruit
4. ears oh job are mouse mark come open all ye faithful
5. all unto soul clip seed their eternal paper deed real cry

_____

_____

Animals Of The Bible Word Search

adder
asp
bear
bee beetle
behemoth
bird
boar
gnat

goat
owl
ox
hen
heron
ram
raven
calf

camel
sparrow
swallow
donkey
dove
turtle dove
eagle
fish

flea
lamb
leopard
lion
locust
whale
wolf

```
N  T  F  B  Y  T  G  H  J  T  A  N  G  U  I  O
A  D  D  E  R  E  X  W  D  Y  N  O  L  M  D  J
N  Y  V  A  S  A  D  L  M  K  E  H  B  G  R  N
H  F  D  R  I  B  O  P  O  L  L  A  I  J  A  N
Y  B  T  V  F  C  X  B  T  A  L  O  G  I  P  U
H  B  Y  L  U  G  N  E  T  H  S  I  F  L  O  P
L  S  O  S  G  F  E  S  A  E  W  E  O  T  E  R
E  W  T  N  T  B  S  P  A  R  R  O  W  N  L  T
F  A  N  U  E  T  E  N  O  O  Y  B  I  M  O  U
F  L  V  E  O  V  L  H  E  N  A  F  M  N  V  R
D  L  B  O  M  I  A  L  E  L  T  L  T  N  B  T
Y  O  E  L  R  D  H  R  A  M  Q  A  M  H  I  L
R  W  E  A  U  N  W  C  R  V  O  C  T  M  E  E
P  L  O  M  G  T  Y  F  E  G  W  T  X  C  E  D
V  R  F  B  G  T  M  U  V  Y  L  T  H  B  I  O
O  L  P  K  Y  E  K  N  O  D  U  B  P  S  A  V
P  C  A  M  E  L  D  F  D  K  D  P  F  M  I  E
```

Tour of the Holy Land

Pastor Smith is leading a tour of the Holy Land, and these are the places he plans to visit:

BETHLEHEM GALILEE
CAESAREA GETHSEMANE
CANA JERICHO
CAPERNAUM JERUSALEM
EMMAUS NAZARETH

Help him with his itinerary by locating all ten places in the chart below by linking adjoining circles. Circles may be joined up, down, forward, backward, or diagonally. Not all circles will be used. **EMMAUS** is done for you...

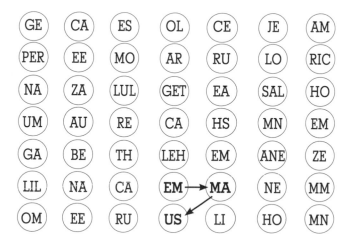

Match Ups

See if you can match each name in the first column with a related word in the second column.

BIBLE PLACES

1. One of the 7 churches in Revelation

2. City defeated by Joshua

3. 10 Commandments site

4. City where Jonah preached

5. Site of Jacob's Ladder dream

6. City of David

7. Home of Amos the prophet

8. Jesus visited here many times

9. Paul led here after his conversion

a. Sinai

b. Smyrna

c. Damascus

d. Jerusalem

e. Tekoa

f. Capernaum

g. Jericho

h. Nineveh

i. Bethel

BIBLE PEOPLE

1. Oldest person

2. Wicked king

3. Good queen

4. Giant

5. Leader out of Egypt

6. Priest

7. Forerunner of Jesus

8. Mother of 6 sons

9. Raised by Peter from the dead

a. Moses

b. Leah

c. John the Baptist

d. Eli

e. Ahab

f. Dorcas

g. Methuselah

h. Goliath

i. Esther

Look Again!

There are 5 subtle differences between these two pictures. Can you find them?

"He's Got the Whole World in His Hands"

Front-Word, Back-Word

The clue in the first column is a word that, read backward, answers the clue in the second column.

1. Magi followed it   _____   An exclamation

2. Morning moisture   _____   Like Abraham and Sarah, for example

3. Hold on to   _____   Sneaked glimpse

4. Commandment number   _____   Fisherman's need

5. Poet   _____   Dull

6. Jesus' cross   _____   Entrance

7. Stairway feature   _____   Dogs and cats, often

8. Fierce battle   _____   Not cooked

9. Pen tip   _____   Container

10. Circle   _____   Bethesda was one

11. Doze   _____   Strips

12. Jonathan to David, for example   _____   Swimmer's distance

13. Insane   _____   Reservoir sight

14. The best!   _____   Stain

Evening Star

See how many 4-letter words you can form by moving from one letter to the next along lines. You can go in any direction the lines go, and you can return to a letter. However, do not skip letters or count a letter twice by staying on it. No plurals!

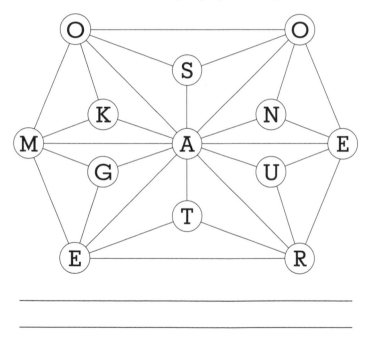

_____

_____

_____

_____

Creation Sings

The Psalmist wrote songs and poems of thanks and praise to God for the majesty of creation. Selecting from the word box below, fill in the blanks with the natural wonder mentioned by the Psalmist.

MOUNTAINS	STARS
TREE	EARTH
SKIES	SUN
FIELD	HEAVEN
EARTH	TREES
EARTH	HILLS
CLOUDS	MOON
HEAVENS	RIVERS
WOOD	SEA
MOON	EARTH
SEAS	

1. When I consider thy _____, the work of thy fingers, the _____ and the _____, which thou has ordained (Psalm 8:3).

2. Let all the _____ fear the LORD (Psalm 33:8).

3. And he shall be like a _____ planted by the _____ of water (Psalm 1:3).

4. He appointed the _____ for seasons: the _____ knoweth his going down (Psalm 104:19).

5. Let the _____ and _____ praise him, the _____, and every thing that moveth therein (Psalm 69:34).

6. Therefore will not we fear, though the _____ be removed, and though the _____ be carried into the midst of the _____ (Psalm 46:2).

7. In his hand are the deep places of the _____: the strength of the _____ is his also (Psalm 95:4).

8. The _____ poured out water: the _____ sent out a sound: thine arrows also went abroad (Psalm 77:17).

9. Let the _____ be joyful, and all that is therein: then shall all the _____ of the _____ rejoice (Psalm 96:12).

Double Meaning

Many words are spelled the same but have different meanings. Write the word that fits both phrases of each quote. When you are finished, the first letter of each word will spell the name of a popular and much-loved saint.

1. I didn't feel **this way**...after paying the **consequence** for my speeding ticket.
2. I'll take my **ease**...for the **remainder** of the day.
3. I'll **talk to** the crowd...from my own **front porch**.
4. Be **civil**...when you visit **this French city**.
5. The entire **acting company**...wore **one** after they broke a leg."
6. Let's talk about the **problem**...with this **magazine**.
7. I'd like to be a **stitcher**...but the plumber's here to unclog the **drains**.

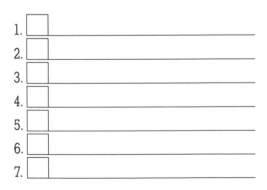

1. ☐ _____
2. ☐ _____
3. ☐ _____
4. ☐ _____
5. ☐ _____
6. ☐ _____
7. ☐ _____

Places Of The Bible
Word Search

Antioch	Damascus	Nazareth
Bethlehem	Emmaus	Tarsus
Caesarea	Ephesus	Tyre
Cana	Joppa	
Capernaum	Jericho	
Corinth	Jerusalem	

```
O L P K I E Y N G B U B H Y V R
P J W S X A M F A K D P F M I P
F E N U G T W M O T A R S U S L
Y R C A P E R N A U M F M N N C
D U W N M I K L P U A G V N A A
Y S T T R D E P H A S U S H Z P
R A E I U N T C R V C D E S A P
N L F O B T G H J L U O M U R O
U E H C V E X H D E S O L M E J
N M V H S E T C U K R H B G T N
H F E S Q N Z H O M L I I J H N
Y B T V I E S W L A L O C I N U
H B Y R G V A F T E D C I H O P
L K O H G F N S Y Q H E R T O R
E C R D T Y A E R A S E A C I K
P L O B G T C F E C W S M C E D
V R F B G T M U J Y N T G B I K
```

Who? What? When? Where?

Choose the correct answer to these Bible questions!

1. **What were the Israelites doing when Moses came down from Mount Sinai?**
   a. Praising God   b. Worshiping a golden calf
   c. Waiting patiently

2. **Where was Paul when he experienced conversion?**
   a. On the road to Damascus   b. At home   c. In the temple

3. **Why did women go out to Jesus' tomb early Sunday morning?**
   a. To plant flowers   b. To visit one another   c. To anoint His body

4. **Who is the main author of Psalms?**
   a. Solomon   b. David   c. Saul

5. **Who told Mary she would have a child?**
   a. A prophet   b. Her physician   c. An angel

6. **What was the reason Mary and Joseph fled with their baby to Egypt?**
   a. King Herod's murderous reign   b. The magi told them to
   c. Their in-laws

7. **Where did John the Baptizer baptize people?**
   a. Pool of Bethesda   b. Sea of Galilee   c. Jordan River

8. **Which of the 12 tribes of Israel was the priestly tribe?**
   a. Dan   b. Asher   c. Levi

9. **Who is called the "weeping prophet"?**
   a. Jeremiah   b. Joshua   c. Joel

10. **What happened to Adam and Eve after the Fall?**
    a. They stayed in the Garden of Eden
    b. They were sent away from Eden   c. They fled to Egypt

11. **Who are the two Old Testament figures taken by God directly to heaven?**
    a. Eve and Ezra   b. Enoch and Elijah   c. Elisha and Eleazar

12. **Where did the writing on the wall take place?**
    a. Jerusalem   b. Damascus   c. Babylon

13. **What happened to Samson after he was captured?**
    a. He was blinded   b. He was flogged then freed
    c. He was sent home

14. **Why was Jonah swallowed by a fish?**
    a. It was an accident   b. He had tried to avoid God's command
    c. The fish was hungry

Echoes of the Bible

Many quotes and phrases commonly used today in conversation and in literature are from the Bible. How many can you identify? Name the speaker or writer; and context.

1. "The greatest of these is love."

   _____

2. "Am I my brother's keeper?"

   _____

3. "The Lord is my shepherd."

   _____

4. "Behold the man!"

   _____

5. "Let my people go!"

   _____

6. "Blessed art thou among women."

   _____

7. "Whither thou goest, I will go."

_____

8. "Do you betray the Son of Man with a kiss?"

_____

9. "How do you know you aren't here for such a time as this?"

_____

10. "You are bone of my bones, flesh of my flesh."

_____

11. "How can I do this great wickedness and sin against God?"

_____

12. "Feed my sheep."

_____

God's Faithfulness

A Bible truth about God's faithfulness can be found from "Let us" by moving from adjoining boxes in any direction, including diagonally.

PROFESSION	THE	FAITH	WITHOUT
OF	OUR	FAST	WAVERING
LET US	HOLD	HE	FOR
PROMISED	THAT	FAITHFUL	IS

Let us _____

_____

_____

_____

_____

An Eventful Journey

Moses led the Children of Israel from Egypt and to the Promised Land. During their 40 years' wandering and before they reached their destination, a lot happened! Put these 12 events in order as they took place in the Bible account:

___ Out of anger, Moses breaks the two tablets of stone given to Him by God. (Exodus 32:19-20)

___ Joshua leads the Israelites across the Jordan River. (Joshua 3:14-17)

___ Aaron makes a golden calf for the people to worship. (Exodus 32:1-4)

___ God sends manna and quail for His people to eat. (Exodus 16:13-15)

___ Joshua sends spies into Canaan. (Joshua 2:1)

___ Moses receives the Commandments a second time. (Exodus 34:28)

___ The Israelites build a tabernacle. (Exodus 39:32)

___ The Israelites celebrate the first Passover. (Exodus 12:1-28)

___ Moses dies. (Deuteronomy 34:5)

___ The Israelites cross the Red Sea on dry land. (Exodus 14:21-22)

___ After 430 years in Egypt, the Israelites depart. (Exodus 12:40-41)

___ Moses receives the Ten Commandments from God. (Exodus 20:1-17)

Stop and Smell the Roses

Consider the lilies how they grow:
they toil not, they spin not.
Luke 12:27

Can you find the 21 flowers they planted?

```
T  O  S  N  A  P  D  R  A  G  O  N  I  N  G
B  E  A  M  S  Z  D  A  F  F  O  D  I  L  I
U  M  Z  S  E  N  E  S  L  I  L  U  R  S  N
T  E  A  U  T  I  V  A  I  N  E  D  R  A  G
T  N  L  M  O  E  O  I  V  I  O  L  E  T  S
A  R  E  C  Q  U  R  L  P  O  R  D  S  I  S
O  C  A  R  N  A  T  I  O  N  H  A  I  A  W
N  P  W  I  T  I  N  G  S  I  R  I  S  E  E
P  E  T  L  L  I  L  Y  E  M  I  S  P  I  E
A  T  U  M  I  N  S  P  A  N  S  Y  E  U  T
Z  U  L  I  A  L  U  M  S  O  E  S  O  N  P
I  N  I  A  S  O  A  L  I  R  I  N  N  S  E
R  I  P  E  N  S  Y  C  P  O  P  P  Y  P  A
M  A  R  I  G  O  L  D  C  S  I  C  O  R  I
U  C  Z  I  N  N  I  A  M  E  N  O  S  I  S
M  A  M  S  S  T  E  N  N  O  B  E  U  L  B
```

Bible Connections

Draw a line from the Bible name to his or her Bible connection!

1. Moses

2. Aaron

3. John the Baptist

4. Lot's wife

5. Judas Iscariot

6. Ezekiel

7. Daniel

8. Shadrach, Meshach, Abednego

9. Belshazzar

10. Job

a. Locusts and wild honey

b. Valley of dry bones

c. Fiery furnace

d. Devastating loss

e. Burning bush

f. Handwriting on the wall

g. Budding staff

h. Lion's den

i. Pillar of salt

j. 30 pieces of silver

Scripture Match Up

Can you match the reference with the phrase or verse?

1. Continue in prayer, and watch in the same with thanksgiving

   Numbers 6:24

2. Trust in the LORD with all thine heart; and lean not unto thine own understanding

   Proverbs 1:5

3. Come unto me, all ye that labour and are heavy laden, and I will give you rest

   Colossians 4:2

4. A wise man will hear, and will increase learning; and a man of understanding shall attain unto wise counsels

   Psalm 27:14

5. Wait on the LORD: be of good courage, and he shall strengthen thine heart

   Proverbs 3:5

6. I am the bread of life: he that cometh to me shall never hunger; and he that believeth on me shall never thirst

   John 6:35

7. The LORD bless thee, and keep thee

   Matthew 11:28

Word Shuffle

From the word list below, select three words that fit into each category. Many words fit in more than one category, but only one arrangement will provide three words for each category. Use each word only once.

ROMANS	SAMUEL	RUTH	MELCHIZEDEK	ESTHER	JUDGES
MATTHEW	EZEKIEL	ELIZABETH	GENESIS	ORPAH	ELIJAH
GALILEE	AHAB	LUKE	NATHANAEL	MARY	GALATIANS
JUDAH	ELI	JOSEPH	ANDREW	REBEKAH	JOHN
CORINTHIANS	GILGAL	HEROD	ANNA	LEAH	PAUL
AMOS	PETER	PSALMS	DANIEL	DAVID	NAOMI

1. Jesus' disciples _____ _____ _____

2. Priests _____ _____ _____

3. Places _____ _____ _____

4. O.T. books _____ _____ _____

5. Epistles _____ _____ _____

6. Brides _____ _____ _____

7. Gospel books _____ _____ _____

8. Mothers _____ _____ _____

9. Kings _____ _____ _____

10. Prophets _____ _____ _____

11. Widows _____ _____ _____

12. Prisoners _____ _____ _____

Word Search

The words in the list below are associated with a familiar parable. Words may read forward, backward, up, down, or diagonally. When you have found all the words in the word search puzzle, the remaining letters will spell out an appropriate title for the parable.

Word List

ALIVE	PIGS	SINS
CALF	RAN	SIRE
FEAST	RING	SKID
FOUND	ROBE	SORRY
GAVE	SAD	STY
ILL	SAY	TWO
IRE	SEAMY	YES
KISS	SERVANT	

```
G  N  I  R  R  T  W  O
P  S  E  R  V  A  N  T
S  R  S  F  S  I  N  S
A  I  O  S  E  A  M  Y
Y  L  N  D  G  A  V  E
F  L  A  C  I  I  S  S
A  L  I  V  E  G  P  T
F  L  S  K  I  D  A  Y
O  O  I  I  S  A  D  L
U  Y  R  S  O  R  R  Y
N  A  E  S  R  O  B  E
D  L  F  A  T  H  E  R
```

Parable Title: _____

Bible Crossword

Across

1. "I once was blind, but now I ___"
4. O.T. false gods
6. To gasp for air
7. Classroom helper (abbr.)
9. Isaac's dad, familiarly
10. Jacob's seventh son
11. "Jesus Loves __"
12. Sacred gemstones
13. Of the moon
15. "Thy ___ and thy staff they comfort me" (Psalm 23:4)

Down

1. Reasonable
2. "We remember the fish, which we did ___ in Egypt" (Numbers 11:5)
3. ___-Shaddai, "God Almighty"
4. O.T. tower
5. Set of steps
6. Cooking spray
8. Org. department
10. One who completed high school (abbr.)
12. Card game
14. Native place to 9 Across

Bible Stars

The letters of three names from the Bible - Dorcas, Mark, Eli - have been dropped into circles inside the star. How many four-letter words can you form by moving along the lines from circle to circle? You cannot skip a letter or count a letter twice, but you can go back to a letter. No capitalized words or plurals allowed. We found 22 words.

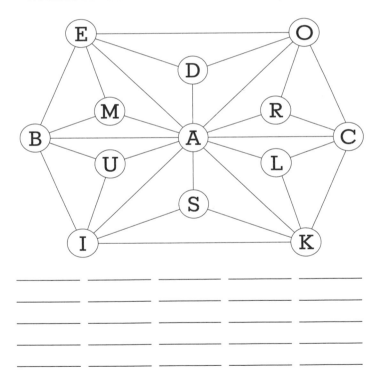

_____ _____ _____ _____ _____
_____ _____ _____ _____ _____
_____ _____ _____ _____ _____
_____ _____ _____ _____ _____
_____ _____ _____ _____ _____

Comparisons

The first part of each statement refers to a certain relationship. To complete the second part, pick the word that follows the same relationship.

**Example: Cain is to Abel as Peter is to <u>Andrew</u>
(two sets of brothers)**

1. David is to king as Felix is to _____.
   a. dictator   b. governor   c. prince   d. servant

2. Peter is to fisherman as Paul is to _____.
   a. tent maker   b. carpenter   c. cook   d. tax collector

3. Genesis is to Moses as Acts is to _____.
   a. Paul   b. Silas   c. Mark   d. Luke

4. Noah is to flood as Shadrach, Meshach and Abednego are to

   _____.
   a. lion's den   b. big fish   c. fiery furnace   d. herbs & spices

5. Elisha is to Elijah as Timothy is to _____.
   a. Paul   b. Apollos   c. Stephen   d. Titus

6. Denial is to Peter as doubt is to _____.
   a. Mark   b. Matthew   c. Thomas   d. Bartholomew

7. Healing is to miracle as sower is to _____.
   a. proverb   b. parable   c. sermon   d. hymn

8. Tree of Life is to Eden as temple is to _____.
   a. Jerusalem   b. synagogue   c. church   d. Judah

What Is It?

Pick the right description for each named object.

1. **BABEL**
a. Mountain
b. Tower
c. Altar

2. **EDEN**
a. Garden
b. Tree
c. Serpent

3. **GOLGOTHA**
a. River
b. Hill
c. Town

4. **EBENEZER**
a. Stone
b. Tree
c. River

5. **JORDAN**
a. Sea
b. Pond
c. River

6. **EPHOD**
a. Rod
b. Temple
c. Garment

7. **GALILEE**
a. Garden
b. Lake
c. Pasture

8. **ADAR**
a. Month
b. Year
c. Day

9. **PRAETORIUM**
a. Arena
b. Hall
c. Roof

10. **BAAL**
a. Haystack
b. Cart
c. Idol

Parents and Children

Match each Bible child with his or her mother!

1. **DINAH**
a. Rachel
b. Leah
c. Sarah

2. **SOLOMON**
a. Bathsheba
b. Elizabeth
c. Delilah

3. **MIRIAM**
a. Rachel
b. Joanna
c. Jochebed

4. **OBED**
a. Esther
b. Ruth
c. Naomi

5. **SETH**
a. Eve
b. Sarah
c. Rebekah

6. **SAMUEL**
a. Mary
b. Hannah
c. Ruth

7. **TIMOTHY**
a. Lois
b. Eunice
c. Dorcas

8. **JAMES**
a. Sarah
b. Joanna
c. Mary

9. **JESUS**
a. Mary
b. Sarah
c. Rebekah

Famous Words

Pick the speaker of each Bible quote!

1. "Am I my brother's keeper?"
   a. Abel   b. Noah   c. Cain

2. "Thou shalt love thy neighbor as thyself."
   a. Jesus   b. Luke   c. Mark

3. "Behold the man!"
   a. Ananias   b. Pilate   c. Herod

4. "Behold the handmaid of the Lord; be it unto me according to thy word."
   a. Mary   b. Dorcas   c. Sarah

5. "Blessed are the peacemakers: for they shall be called the children of God."
   a. Paul   b. John   c. Jesus

6. "Silver and gold have I none; but such as I have give I thee."
   a. Jesus   b. Peter   c. John

7. "If I perish, I perish."
   a. Delilah   b. Deborah   c. Esther

Bible Combos

Combine letter groups from columns 1, 2 and 3 (in that order) to form books of the Bible. Each group will be used only once. The first one has been done for you.

1	2	3
SA	ADI	UA
CO	OVE	ON
TI	CHAR	EL
OB	GG	WS
CHR	MU	RBS
JO	LATI	HY
PR	TH	CLES
PHI	BRE	IAH
HA	MOT	AI
GA	LEM	ER
HE	RINT	ANS
ES	ONI	AH
ZE	SH	HIANS

Samuel

_____

_____

_____

_____

_____

_____

_____

_____

_____

_____

_____

_____

Who said it?

Match the rhyme with the speaker, using the list of names in the box below:

PAUL   PETER   MARTHA
ANNA   SARAH   DAVID
SIMEON   RUTH   NOAH

A. I swore I'd be loyal no matter what came—
   But instead I denied Him, and felt bitter shame.

   _____

B. As Abraham's wife and late in my life,
   I held my first son at ninety and one!

   _____

C. In the temple we saw Him—our Messiah and Lord!
   He was born as God promised and prophets foretold!

   _____

D. I slew a tough giant with a stone and a sling,
And was later anointed as Israel's king.

_____

E. Of resurrected Jesus, I would have no part
Until the Holy Spirit changed my hardened heart.

_____

F. I'm glad I obeyed—though far from the sea,
The ark that I built saved my family and me!

_____

G. I stayed with Naomi and went to her land,
Then soon Boaz saw me and asked for my hand.

_____

H. My sister sat by Him and listened
instead of helping me serve food—
The Lord said I was way too busy,
and Mary chose the greater good.

_____

Bible Crossword Puzzle

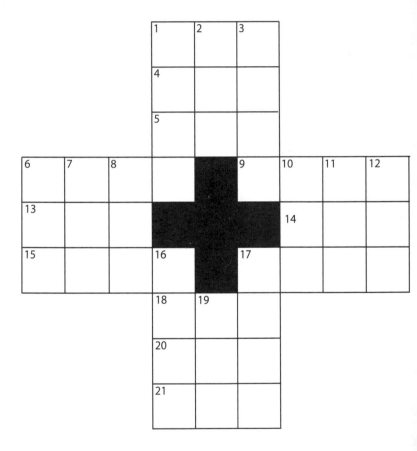

ACROSS

1. Hannah's priest (1 Sam. 1:9)
4. Luke was one, for short (Col. 4:14)
5. Deer relative
6. Cut of meat
9. Thread from Egypt (2 Chr. 1:16)
13. There was no room in one (Luke 2:7)
14. Bring legal action against
15. Ruth's husband (Ruth 4:13)
17. Rave's partner
18. Adam's partner (Gen. 3:20)
20. Swift deer (Prov. 6:5)
21. Night hooter

DOWN

1. Residence of 18 Across (Gen. 2:8)
2. E-mail acronym
3. Describes day-old manna (Exo. 16:20)
6. Women's ___, feminist movement
7. Town built by the sons of Elpaal (1 Chr. 8:12)
8. "Lead me __ __ plain path" (Psa. 27:11)
10. King of Judah (1 Kings 15:8)
11. What you should do from temptation
12. Peter cast it into the sea (Matt. 4:18)
16. Number before one
17. Holds fishing line
19. Solemn promise

Signs, Symbols, and Astonishing Sights

In the Bible, God appeared in many ways. Here are just a few of them!

ACROSS

1 God spoke to him in a burning bush

4 Angel Gabriel brought God's message to this young girl

5 God inflicted 10 plagues upon this nation to reveal His power

8 Abraham and Sarah's late-in-life son

10 God spoke to him in a still, small voice

12 Confusion of languages tower

13 Event that proved Jesus' victory over death

17 God put a star in the sky to lead them

18 Zechariah and Elizabeth's late-in-life son

19 God created this garden for Adam and Eve

20 God prepared a great fish to swallow this reluctant prophet

DOWN

2 Lot's wife turned into a pillar of __

3 God gave him the power to interpret the handwriting on the wall

6 Jesus walked on the water on this sea

7 Holy Spirit appeared as this at Jesus' baptism

9 God gave him the power to defeat Goliath

11 God gave him the power to crumble Jericho's walls

14 God told him to build an ark to survive the Flood

15 Holy Spirit appeared as tongues of __ at Pentecost

16 Along with five loaves and two of these, Jesus fed 5000

17 God sent this from heaven to feed the Children of Israel as they wandered in the desert

Lift Up Your Heart

Find the highlighted words below.

Ask, and it shall be given you;
seek, and ye shall find; **knock**,
and it shall be **opened** unto you.

Matthew 7:7

I **sought** the Lord, and he **heard** me,
and **delivered** me from all **my fears**.

Psalm 34:4

He shall **call upon** me, and I will **answer** him:
I will be with him in trouble;
I will deliver him, and **honour** him.

Psalm 91:15

```
W  Z  C  K  K  N  O  C  K  S  F  D  R  A  E  H
J  E  P  R  A  S  Y  Z  I  J  O  D  Q  U  P  N
L  D  U  N  D  N  J  Y  N  G  L  U  Q  F  X  Z
I  J  E  K  V  Y  B  Y  Z  L  Q  J  G  R  K  X
T  K  T  L  T  W  H  K  W  E  O  C  P  H  W  O
P  K  R  D  I  E  S  K  T  O  S  X  R  I  T  C
M  L  R  R  M  V  A  M  J  S  H  Q  I  R  A  D
Y  D  A  E  W  W  E  R  L  A  R  I  Y  L  S  N
T  H  C  R  Q  O  T  R  U  Z  X  A  L  A  A  S
L  E  G  H  F  W  U  O  E  W  D  U  E  L  A  K
J  O  P  E  N  E  D  M  H  D  P  C  L  F  L  K
I  X  X  J  E  U  X  Z  S  O  E  E  Q  N  Y  F
Y  K  P  X  P  U  H  U  N  C  T  F  S  N  N  M
Q  E  A  C  W  R  U  N  I  Y  X  V  V  J  R  H
T  T  S  G  U  D  H  L  P  Q  R  K  E  E  S  N
S  B  V  O  T  W  R  Y  P  S  A  E  N  O  J  O
J  E  N  Y  Y  O  M  K  K  S  R  R  W  U  A  U
E  O  M  R  Z  A  W  F  W  B  E  T  J  S  P  Q
H  U  E  M  Q  J  Z  Q  Q  W  P  J  N  M  N  T
J  D  T  B  N  R  B  R  K  K  U  M  I  J  P  A
```

Transformations

Faith is life-changing because God changes lives. Follow the path of these word pairs to transform them. Change the first word into the last word of each pair by replacing only one letter at a time. Do not scramble letter order, use only common English words, and no capitalized words.

Example: LOSE, lone, line, fine, FIND

1. HURT
   _____
   _____
   _____
   _____
   CALM

2. FEAR
   _____
   _____
   _____
   _____
   PRAY

3. STAY
   _____
   _____
   _____
   _____
   FREE

4. REAL
   _____
   _____
   _____
   _____
   _____
   LIFE

5. TRUE
   _____
   _____
   _____
   _____
   _____
   _____
   LOVE

Words Matter

The world has enough critics, but it can always use champions who think about what other people might be going through... to listen to another person's perspective...to ask, "Can I help?" Follow the clues below by crossing off the words in the grid. Some words might be crossed off by more than one clue. When you are finished, the remaining words form a saying, reading left to right.

1. Cross off all names of colors.
2. Cross off all words that rhyme with pan.
3. Cross off all foods and beverages.
4. Cross off all words containing two sets of double letters.
5. Cross off all words that are names of flowers or trees.
6. Cross off all words that contain the word ant.

MILK	TWO	BUTTRESS	PLAN
THINGS	ROSE	ARE	GRANT
BAD	TEAL	CAN	FOR
COMMITTED	THE	PIE	PURPLE
HEART	OAK	RUNNING	PALM
UPSTAIRS	YELLOW	AND	RUNNING
PLEASANT	DOWN	AZURE	POMEGRANATE
SPAN	CORN	PEOPLE	ABBESS

Saying: _____

Who Follows Jesus Word Search

The names below are just a few of Jesus' followers as recorded in the Bible. Find their names hidden forward, backward, horizontally, vertically and diagonally.

ANDREW
APOLLOS
AQUILA
BARNABAS
BARTHOLOMEW
CHILDREN
CORNELIUS
ETHIOPIAN
JAMES
JOHN
JUDE
JULIA
LUKE
LYDIA
MARK
MARY
MATTHEW
NICODEMUS

PAUL
PETER
PHILEMON
PHILIP
PHOEBE
PRISCILLA
SAINTS
SILAS
SIMON
SINNERS
STEPHEN
TABITHA
THIEF
THOMAS
TIMOTHY
TITUS
YOU
ZACCHEUS

```
U A B N E D B G C C G X D R X R F H F A A T
L P X S I E K U L A K X I V L S R E N N I S
U J S O Z C K J H A D Y V Z C X R V L M M H
A T T C F W O T U F Q K H V C M G U O P U A
P H E I I T I D T D H U I O T N H T R N P S
Q O P K A B E C E I E W I A D R H I Q O J U
H M H U A O S T H M T V U L I Y S D L A U I
Z A E T G Z Y C H P U U P B A C J L M X L L
X S N B W H E V R I I S S E I X O O T X I E
D D C I A B G U P W O U O L T S J D W R A N
H C T D E R S N T K Y P L Y Z W H B O C G R
A H X O A C T Z M I K A I W Y E H L R O Q O
R N H F R U P H I L I P Z A Y R C R D N D C
U P M X K Z W L O B P J M A N D J M F H A D
Q R D P P V N K V L N H O I X N V I A F F S
F W N X J O H N V S O D A L X A Q F E I H T
W Z E A I D Y L U Q U M Y T J T F A E G E L
P M J M Y C K E U F Z I E W B M D S A L I S
Y E K N I Z H E L O T F E W X R N O M I S U
I P T V E C L J T E Z H L C W O D P Y S M H
S F P E C R A H U F T M L T N C S T N I A S
S I V A R M D L M T P P B K N O M E L I H P
L M Z F E E S L A I B W R R X Y Y N J N M E
E A R S Z L K M I L U R U A S T E R N V Q O
D S A R Q X J B K H L O C M I B V M A M E C
R T B A R N A B A S C A Y G C X N R Q M C O
```

Broaden Your Horizons!

Oh that thou wouldest bless me indeed, and enlarge my coast, and that thine hand might be with me, and that thou wouldest keep me from evil, that it may not grieve me! And God granted him that which he requested.
Prayer of Jabez, 1 Chronicles 4:10

Have you ever been hesitant to apply for a job? Try out for a team? Wonder if you can dance, sing, be happier? Give yourself a chance to explore something new. In this puzzle, you may discover many things you'd like to try!

ACROSS
1 Swift animals
5 Scott Joplin compositions
9 Visual
11 Zion National Park state
12 Singer's voice, maybe
13 Call
14 You might want to sail it
15 M.S. evaluator
17 Commanded
18 Lifts
20 You can strum one
22 Friend
23 Chicago's transport, for short
24 Beret
27 Exits
29 Comment on
31 Old Testament book
32 Accra's locale
33 Make reference to
34 Female 1 Across

DOWN
1 You can connect them
2 Fencer's sword
3 Gas burner
4 __ Grande
5 Join a marathon, e.g.
6 Dickens' "__ of Two Cities" (2 wds.)
7 Sports
8 Outbuilding, maybe
10 Invent
16 Conversation

DOWN Cont'd

18 East Coast state (Abbr.)
19 Jr.'s dad
20 Netting
21 Supreme (Prefix)
22 Verse
24 "Bye-bye"

25 Jesus' grandmother,
   by tradition
26 Legumes
28 __ Francisco
30 Advanced degree

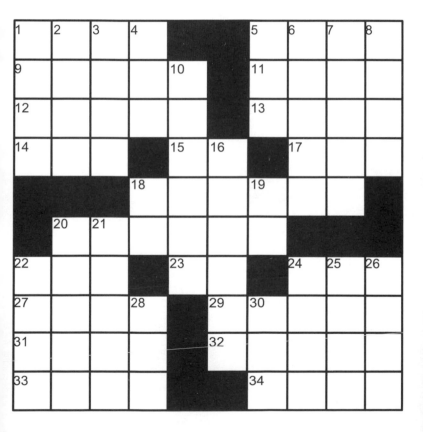

Transformations

Change isn't always easy, But remember this: God never changes. His love is the same yesterday, today, and forever!

Change the first word into the last word of each pair by replacing only one letter at a time. Do not scramble letter order; use only common English words, and no capitalized words.

Example:
LOSE, lone, line, fine, FIND

3. LESS

1. TINY

_____

_____

_____

_____

VAST

_____

_____

_____

_____

MORE

4. MEAN

2. POOR

_____

_____

_____

_____

_____

KIND

_____

_____

_____

_____

_____

RICH

5. HOLD

_____

_____

_____

_____

_____

GIVE

Missions Accomplished

Match the name of the Bible leader in the first column with the event in the second column.

1. David

A. Led an army against the fearsome Canaanites and defeated them.

2. Abraham

B. Demanded that Pharaoh let God's people leave Egypt.

3. Deborah

C. Lived in the desert and preached repentance to the people.

4. Paul

D. Took on a hardened warrior, though a youth and armed only with a stone.

5. Ananias

E. Sent by God to preach repentance to the Ninevites, even though he was reluctant to do so.

6. Esther

F. Endured imprisonment and floggings, yet continued to preach the Gospel message.

7. Moses

8. Joseph

G. Married his pregnant fiancée because God told him in a dream that she would give birth to Jesus.

H. Uprooted his household and set out for a land promised to him by God.

9. John

10. Jonah

I. Approached a known persecutor of the early church because God told him to do so.

J. Risked her life to save her people from a genocidal plot.

Timely Matters

All the answers in this puzzle are related to time.

ACROSS

3 Timeless
5 "One day is with the Lord as a thousand __..." (2 Peter 3:8)
9 "Teach us to __ our days" (Psa. 90:12)
11 "Time is __," says the starter
13 "Time is __," says the boss
16 __ Saving Time
17 "Time __," says the harried one
18 Calendar heading

DOWN

1 "In __time," says the procrastinator
2 "A time of war, a time of __" (Eccl. 3:8)
4 "Time and __ wait for no man"
6 "It's __ time!" sighs the impatient one
7 "A time to every __ under the heaven" (Eccl. 3:1)
8 "Time and __ happeneth to them all" (Eccl. 9:11)
10 "The LORD will deliver him in time of __" (Psa. 41:1)
12 "Time heals all __"
14 "Time is too __," says the busy one
15 Time keeper

Big Puzzler

Relax and enjoy solving this modern day crossword puzzle!

ACROSS

1 Affirms
6 South American nation
10 Big __, London landmark
13 Limited
15 Cry of dismay
16 Paris street
17 New Testament Roman ruler
18 Ride the waves
19 Fall mo.
20 Gardener's medium
22 Fill with joy
24 Jesus, the __ Shepherd
26 Operator
28 Challenge
29 Damage
30 Happy
31 Filleted
32 Pie __ mode (2 words)
33 Swift
34 Computer keyboard key
35 Tropical malady
37 Have
41 Movie scene
42 Canter
43 Deer cousin
44 Tent fastener
47 Winged
48 Work's opposite
49 Domicile
50 Word book (Abbr.)
51 Fastener
52 Creative products
54 Seers
56 English title
57 River dam
59 Resurrection Day
63 Beverage
64 Zilch
65 Formal agreement
66 Query
67 Air pollution
68 Ceasefire

DOWN

1 Athletic org.
2 By way of
3 Solo
4 What Solomon had
5 Sedate
6 Dads
7 Got away from
8 Less common
9 '80s athletic org.
10 Coarse ankle-high work shoe
11 Card game
12 Got as profit

DOWN CON'T
14 Sin
21 City in Oklahoma
23 Baals
24 Big celebration
25 Spoken
27 Rested
29 Noah's son
30 Stride
31 Top-notch
33 Without cost
34 Portal
36 Crooked
37 Chatter
38 Snaky fish
39 Strike

40 Heavens
42 Nurse's trait, for short
44 Cascade mountain
45 Early American British supporters
46 Commuter train company
47 Japanese martial art
48 Quarterback
50 Imagine
51 Chest thumper
53 Has
55 Still
58 Cleaning cloth
60 Greek letter
61 List ender
62 Bread choice

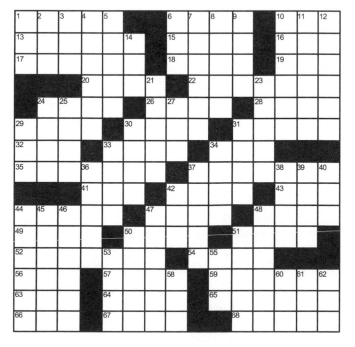

Decode the Quote

Fill in the words that match their definitions. Then, complete the solution by placing each letter that corresponds with its matching number into the spaces below. When you're finished, you'll find what president ABRAHAM LINCOLN had to say about prayer.

Skin

__	__	__	__	__	__
8	5	9	10	1	13

Scowl

__	__	__	__	__	__
18	17	14	16	5	9

Bulb blossom

__	__	__	__	__
12	20	17	1	21

Convoy

___ ___ ___ ___ ___ ___ ___
19   3   9   3   4   3   7

Schmooze

___ ___ ___ ___ ___ ___
2   14   6   7   14   6

What an eggwhite omelet lacks

___ ___ ___ ___
11   14   17   15

1		2	3	4	5		6	5	5	7		8	9	1	4	5	7			
10	3	7	11		12	1	10	5	13		12	14		10	11					
																—				
15	7	5	5	13		6	11		12	2	5		14	4	5	9				
16	2	5	17	10	1	7	18		19	14	7	4	1	19	12	1	14	7		
12	2	3	12		1		2	3	8		3	6	13	14	17	20	12	5	17	11
																				.
7	14		14	12	2	5	9		21	17	3	19	5		12	14		18	14	

Rhyme Time

Each clue can be answered with two rhyming words. All refer to a well-known Bible figure, and the spaces show how many letters are in the answer. Example:

Adam's son's great canines = **CAIN'S DANES**

1. First woman's wheat bundles

___ ___ ___ ___ '___   ___ ___ ___ ___ ___ ___ ___

2. Gospel writer's English noblemen

___ ___ ___ ___ '___   ___ ___ ___ ___ ___

3. Ark builder's feathery scarves

___ ___ ___ ___ '___   ___ ___ ___ ___

4. Naomi's faithful daughter-in-law's small enclosures

___ ___ ___ ___ '___   ___ ___ ___ ___ ___ ___

5. Moses' brother's long-legged wading birds

___ ___ ___ ___ ___ '___   ___ ___ ___ ___ ___ ___

6. Gospel writer's green spaces

___ ___ ___ ___ '___   ___ ___ ___ ___ ___

7. Epistle writer's fairground shelters

___ ___ ___ ___ '___   ___ ___ ___ ___ ___ ___

8. The Baptizer's young deer

___ ___ ___ ___ '___   ___ ___ ___ ___ ___

All in the Family

Get acquainted with these Bible families! Match the description in the first column with the family member in the second column.

1. Jesus often visited the Bethany home of Mary and Martha and their brother.

   A. Peter

2. This beloved son of King David connived to take his father's throne.

   B. John

3. Jesus healed this disciple's mother-in-law's fever.

   C. Ruth

4. In the very first family, this son murdered his brother, Abel.

   D. Solomon

5. Their jealousy led his eleven brothers to sell him into slavery.

   E. Sarah

6. Leaving their father Zebedee's fishing business, James and his brother went to follow Jesus.

   F. Cain

7. King David's son with Bathsheba was renowned for his wisdom and wealth.

   G. Moses

8. This missionary followed his mother Eunice and grandmother Lois in the faith.

   H. Joseph

9. Abraham's wife bore a son, Isaac, late in life.

   I. Timothy

10. This faithful daughter-in-law left her own land to go with her widowed mother-in-law, Naomi.

    J. Lazarus

11. His brother Aaron spoke for him in front of Pharaoh of Egypt.

    K. Absalom

Funny Money

Our view of money reflects our relationship with God and those around us. God promises, "Seek ye first the kingdom of God, and his righteousness; and all these things shall be added unto you." (Matthew 6:33).
See if you know the answer to these money questions!

1. According to records, who guarded the first U.S. Mint in Philadelphia?
   a. Watchdog b. 2 Soldiers c. It wasn't guarded

2. If you stack 48 pennies, how high would your stack be?
   a. 1″ b. 2″ c. 3″

3. About how much was the price of a gallon of gas in 1950?
   a. 15¢ b. 25¢ c. 35¢

4. The first non-mythical person to appear on a regular-issue U.S. coin was President Lincoln in 1909. Who was the first non-mythical woman to appear?
   a. Martha Washington
   b. Susan B. Anthony
   c. Queen Isabella of Spain

5. What dollar denomination is a Benjamin?
   a. $50 b. $100 c. $500

6. Approximately how much does the average American spend on fast food annually?
   a. $1,200 b. $2,200 c. $3,200

7. What percent of income is a literal tithe?
   a. 5% b. 10% c. 15%

8. During which war did the United States first start printing bills?
   a. Revolutionary War
   b. Spanish-American War
   c. Civil War

9. How much does it cost to produce a nickel?
   a. Less than it costs to produce a dime
   b. More than it costs to produce a dime
   c. About the same as it costs to produce a dime

10. About how long does a dollar bill last in circulation?
    a. Less than 6 years
    b. More than 10 years
    c. Only one year

Flower Show

The flowers appear on the earth;
the time of the singing of birds is come.
Song of Solomon 2:12

Unscramble the letters for a list of favorite flowers. Then unscramble the letters in parenthesis for another colorful flower, and you'll have a full bouquet!

1. A A T N O N R C I

__ __ __ __ __ __ (__) __ __

2. L F D F D O A I

__ (__) __ __ __ __ __ __

3. S O G L U I D L A

__ __ __ (__) __ __ __ __ __

4. P A A G R O D N S N

(__)__ __ __ __ __ __ __ __

5. S A N Y P   __ __ __ (__) __

6. Z L E A A A   __ __ __ __ (__) __

7. H D I A A L   __ __ __ __ (__) __

Answer: __ __ __ __ __ __ __

Prayer Power

Many of the words in this puzzle are related to prayer.

ACROSS

1 Truth
5 Prep school (Abbr.)
9 Uninvolved
11 "Thy will be ___" (Matt. 6:10)
12 Child-bearer
13 Avant-garde art movement
14 Joppa to Jerusalem dir.
15 Computer memory unit
17 Commandments number
18 Tan colors
20 How Solomon judged
22 Sect.
23 Providence locale (Abbr.)
24 Early patriot's descendent, perhaps
27 "Deliver us from ___" (Matt. 6:13)
29 "Make a joyful ___ unto the LORD" (Psa. 100:1)
31 4-wheeler
32 "Ask, and it shall be ___ you" (Matt. 7:7)
33 Org.
34 "___ us not into temptation" (Matt. 6:13)

DOWN

1 Renown
2 "___! and Did My Savior Bleed?" hymn title
3 "Thy kingdom ___" (Matt. 6:10)
4 Cat
5 Total
6 Raccoon-like animal
7 South American mountain range
8 College head
10 "Our ___," prayer opening (Matt. 6:9)
16 Making bundles of hay
18 Topeka locale (Abbr.)
19 Paducah locale (Abbr.)
20 Leah and Rachel to Jacob
21 Crawling vines
22 ___ vu
24 Swimming pool jump
25 Not ashore
26 "A time to ___, and a time to sew" (Eccl. 3:7)
28 Hosp. staffer
30 "Thou anointest my head with ___" (Psa. 23:5)

It All Adds Up!

Find the word each of the three clues have in common. Write it in the blank to the right. These three solutions form a fourth vertical puzzle. The numbers indicate the number of letters in each solution word. The + tells you the word's position.

For example: + **mate**, + **food** and **lost** + is **SOUL**.

mast +   (4)   _____+
+ quarters
+ phones

thresh +   (4)   + _____
+ up
with +

lunch +   (3)   + _____
chatter +
boom +

Final Answer: (6)   _____

Hint: 2 Corinthians 12:10

Good Words

Words of encouragment and self-forgiveness go a long way toward freeing you from feelings of shame and inferiority. Pick the definition that best fits the "good word".

1. EFFERVESCENT
a. Kind
b. Lively
c. Nice

2. INTREPID
a. Courageous
b. Gentle
c. Agreeable

3. ESTEEMED
a. Essential
b. Honored
c. Nurturing

4. ETHICAL
a. Enthusiastic
b. Secure
c. Principled

5. COMMENDABLE
a. Worthy
b. Intelligent
c. Poised

6. PROLIFIC
a. Productive
b. Friendly
c. Clean

7. EMPATHETIC
a. Powerful
b. Zealous
c. Understanding

8. HUMANITARIAN
a. Compassionate
b. Fun
c. Popular

9. CONTEMPLATIVE
a. Contented
b. Reflective
c. Graceful

10. MUNIFICENT
a. Distinguished
b. Generous
c. Lucid

Abundance Abounds

Your God is a God of huge harvest.

Here's a puzzle designed around the theme of abundance.

ACROSS

1 Significant
3 Outstanding; awesome
9 Big-hearted
11 Hope for
12 Limitless
14 Crop
16 Riches
17 Bestow
20 __-of-the-crop
21 "He which soweth
   bountifully shall __ also
   bountifully"
   (2 Cor. 9:6)
22 Big
23 Satisfied
25 Ask God
27 Awe-struck
28 Gives aid to
29 Present

DOWN

2 "My cup runneth __"
   (Psa. 23:5)
4 Surpass
5 Lush; abundant
6 "Ask what I shall __ thee"
   (1 Kings 3:5)
7 Ample
8 Advantages
10 Bring to
11 Continual
13 "There shall be __ of
   blessing" (Eze. 34:26)
15 Choicest
17 Unearned mercy
18 Show favor to
19 Lots
24 Most pleasant
26 Reap

151

Happy Discoveries

Delight thyself also in the LORD:
and he shall give thee the desires of thine heart.

Psalm 37:4

Put the answer to Clue 1 in box 1. Scramble the letters and drop one letter to answer Clue 2. Write the word in box 2 and the dropped letter in the left-hand box. Scramble the letters and drop one letter to answer Clue 3. Write the word in box 3 and the dropped letter in the right-hand box. Complete each row the same way, starting with a new word. When you're finished, you'll discover two new words reading vertically on both sides of the puzzle. The first line is already done for you.

1. Bed needs	9. Box
2. Not those	10. Citrus
3. KJV pronoun	11. Yard burrower
4. Small field rodent	12. One of the Three Stooges
5. A few	13. Weepy
6. Fruct- or gluc- ending	14. Price
7. Ankle ailment, maybe	15. Pothole filler
8. Couples	

S	*sheets* 1.	*these* 2.	*thee* 3.	S
	4.	5.	6.	
	7.	8.	9.	
	10.	11.	12.	
	13.	14.	15.	

Active Contentment

This is the day which the LORD hath made; we will rejoice and be glad in it.
Psalm 118:24

Many words are spelled the same, but have different meanings, and sometimes different pronunciations. In each sentence below, replace the bolded words with one word. Example:

Her manager was **satisfied** with the **substance** of her report.
Answer: **content**

1. It was a **pleasant** day until he got a **ticket** for speeding.
   Answer: _____

2. He's the **only one** who had to repair the **bottom** of his shoe.
   Answer: _____

3. She didn't feel **fit** when she looked into the **mineshaft**, so the event didn't go **satisfactorily**.
   Answer: _____

4. "It's only **just**," she said as we walked around the arts and crafts **show**.
   Answer: _____

5. I saw her **curtsy** on the **front** of the ship.
   Answer: _____

6. Do you have a **clue** about the group that he **facilitated**?
   Answer: _____

7. Some of the coffee I **milled** spilled all over the **lawn**.
   Answer: _____

8. It was on the **edge** of her tongue to say we should leave a more generous **gratuity**.
   Answer: _____

9. Who wants to **abandon** the group in the Mohave **sands**?
   Answer: _____

10. Despite the cold **breeze**, I continued to **meander** around the garden and **coil** the hose.
    Answer: _____

11. He **stood up** from his chair and gave her a red **flower**.
    Answer: _____

Attention!

Being aware...seeing...hearing...bring new dimensions to a routine, ordinary day. Many clues in this puzzle are designed to get your attention!

ACROSS
1 Hand holder
4 Couple
5 Some time back
6 Time piece
9 Loch __ monster
13 Vase
14 Affirmative
15 High schooler
17 Desire
18 "Three persons, __ God"
20 Promise
21 "Our Father who __ in heaven"

DOWN
1 Esther's month
2 Floor covering
3 Night light
6 Shelter
7 Miner's goal
8 French number
10 View
11 Notice
12 Downhearted
16 Shining star
17 Salamander
19 Neither's partner

Weather Forecast

Match the biblical weather event with the person or place involved.

1. There was a storm on the Sea of Galilee...

2. The sun turned dark...

3. It rained 40 days and nights...

4. A windstorm brought tongues of fire...

5. A windstorm brought a plague of locusts...

6. A great wind tore mountains and shattered rocks...

7. An earthquake dislodged a great stone...

8. Hot sun and wind, after a worm withered a shady plant...

a. ...and the Holy Spirit descended upon the disciples.

b. ...but Noah and his family were safe in the ark.

c. ...but Pharaoh would not let the children of Israel leave Egypt.

d. ...but the Lord was not in it, but in a still, small voice.

e. ...and Jonah was angry with God because of his discomfort.

f. ...and the disciples saw Jesus walk on water.

g. ...and women found not Jesus, but an empty tomb.

h. ...and Jesus died.

Games We Play

I have finished my course, I have kept the faith.
2 Timothy 4:7

Challenge yourself to pick the right answer for these sports-related questions!

1. In which sport would you hear the terms "stale fish" and "mule kick" used?
   a. Skiing
   b. Swimming
   c. Snowboarding

2. Where was Super Bowl I played?
   a. Los Angeles, California
   b. Atlanta, Georgia
   c. Green Bay, Wisconsin

3. What is the maximum amount of time a golfer can look for a lost ball?
   a. 2 min. b. 3 min.
   c. 5 min.

4. In 1994, why was there no baseball World Series?
   a. Players were on strike
   b. Coaches were on strike
   c. Hot dog vendors were on strike

5. Which sport did George Washington play with his troops?
   a. Kickball
   b. Soccer
   c. Cricket

6. When was the Indianapolis Motor Speedway for car racing built?
   a. 1909 b. 1929 c. 1939

7. In the modern Olympic games, when were women first admitted as athletes?
   a. 1886 b. 1900 c. 1904

8. When was the first Wimbledon tennis tournament held?
   a. 1802 b. 1877 c. 1905

Flower Garden

He hath made every thing beautiful in his time.
Ecclesiastes 3:11

Crocus

Daffodil

Tulip

Hyacinth

Bluebell

Dahlia

Amaryllis

Peony

Geranium

Garden rose

Sweet pea

Delphinium

Morning glory

Primrose

Freesia

Pansy

Hydrangea

Poppy

Orchid

Marigold

Iris

Daisy

```
H Y D R A N G E A P O Y G
N J Z M U I N I H P L E D
Z N H Y A C I N T H L D M
Q P P Y L O O Y Y J C A F
A I B E S O R N E D R A G
C L X A E H E U J I X Y D
N U X U J A M R G J C A Y
Y T D A I S Y O F Z F N S
R S I R I B L Y F F V W S
O S A F P D U S O D E T X
L X V X A Q A D X E D H U
G A P U M M I I T W E A E
G S A D A L U P S E W K T
N U N A R R E I S E D X E
I C S H Y A Y O N I E G F
N O Y L L R R P H A A R E
R R N I L M I C P B R R F
O C O A I C R K V O P E E
M B E R S O T Z X M P L G
E A P J I L L E B E U L B
```

Solutions

All problems, even the toughest you face, have one good thing in common – each is an invitation to grow more...pray more...and lean more on God. Unscramble the following solution-focused words, and when you are finished, unscramble the letters in parenthesis for another important point.

1. K H N I T   L L R Y E C A

___ ___ ___ ___ ___   ___ ___ ___ (___) ___ ___ ___

2. E S E R A R H C

(___) ___ ___ ___ ___ ___ ___ ___

3. O T I C J V B I T Y E

___ ___ ___ ___ ___ ___ ___ ___ ___ ___ (___)

4. R S N T E N D C I M E

___ ___ ___ ___ (___) ___ ___ ___ ___ ___ ___

5. R O T O   U S E C A

(___) ___ ___ ___   ___ ___ ___ ___ ___

6. N N N L G P A I

(___) ___ ___ ___ ___ ___ ___ ___

Solution: ___ ___ ___ ___ ___ ___

Awesome People

Match these Bible people with their actions of compassion and faith.

1. She showed compassion and commitment to her mother-in-law, Naomi, by leaving her own land to follow Naomi to Bethlehem.

   a. Joseph

2. He readily forgave his brothers for having sold him into slavery when he was a youth.

   b. David

3. She demonstrated faith by believing the angel Gabriel's message that she would bear the Son of God.

   c. Paul

4. Despite a shipwreck, imprisonment, and other hardships, he persevered in spreading the Gospel message.

   d. Jesus

5. He obeyed God's command to prepare for a great flood, even though there was no rain in sight.

   e. Esther

6. She risked her own life to appear before the Persian king unbidden and implement a plan to save her people from Haman's wicked plot.

   f. Lydia

7. Once his great sin was pointed out to him, he turned to God in heartfelt penitence.

   g. Ruth

8. She provided generous hospitality to the missionaries who brought her the Gospel message.

   h. Noah

9. He made the ultimate sacrifice in atonement for the sins of the world.

   I. Mary

Biblically Named Locals Word Search

One of the oldest churches in America, is the First Church in Salem, MA, founded in 1629.

The places listed below are found in the Bible, as well as the good ol' U.S.A.. Search for the place names written forward, backward, horizontally, vertically and diagonally.

ANTIOCH
ARARAT
BETHANY
BETHEL
BETHESDA
BETHLEHEM
BETHPAGE
CALVARY
CANA
CANAAN
CARMEL
CORINTH
DAMASCUS
EMMAUS
EPHESUS
GALATIA
GOSHEN

HEBRON
ISRAEL
JERICHO
JERUSALEM
JORDAN RIVER
LEBANON
MOAB
MOUNT OLIVE
MOUNT ZION
NAZARETH
OPHIR
PALESTINE
PATMOS
REHOBOTH
SALEM
SHILOH
SHUSHAN
TYRE

```
T V S T T Z D D N O Z A C V G W J J K B P F
W S C P X I X G K R N P A U M Y J G J P U F
P H J A R N K W H T E M N M E H E L H T E B
B U X T J A C O I O S H A X C X P R Z G N L
P S B M E T L O W I E L O F R G R J K S A A
T H H O O I C R E A T J D B N I E V C R A J
K A N S H H S B M T J J G J O R H A J Y N O
P N H S N O I Z T N U O M N I T L P R X A I
S E S N H F U L T S T Y S C O V H R O F C I
U G I A C J S X K M T Y H N A R G N T H E Z
S A S V L N Y E L B A O C R J U B E E N V G
E P T U T E V X J A E G Y C U P E E I H F N
H H J G R S M N V C F L O B V O G T H K C C
P T Z D H E E G A N E R A R A D S E H T E B
E E G O R H B R B H I E B S L E M Z M G D H
R B K A S P M Q T N D P M T L O T J M K L P
E E S O L E W E T C W E M A A X D A B L G B
V Q G Y L A B H M O V C P B J P X K R L W D
I H C Z Y C T S E I V S J M B U L S D A F X
R T N Q O C F I L R U Z N Y B Q V E B C R L
N E K Y G I I O A C Y D U N S E Z G A X W A
A R U U Y U T N S M S T I A U R F N I R J P
D A A V Y N U A U V P U D H A S Z B D Y S R
R Z P M U Z M A R E U P V T M P R G T L T I
O A W O W A L F E X H Q D E M T H E R F B A
J N M G D C P D J T A U J B E N O N A B E L
```

It All Adds Up!

Find the word each of the three clues have in common. Write it in the blank to the right. These three solutions form a fourth vertical puzzle. The numbers indicate the number of letters in each solution word. The + tells you the word' position.

For example: + **mate**, + **food** and **lost** + is **SOUL**.

+ dog   (5)   _____ +
+ word
wrist +

+ break   (6)   _____+
black +
+ house

+ setter   (4)   _____+
out +
+ car

Final Answer: (5)   _____

Hint: God is yours.

Matching Pairs

The Golden Rule teaches us to "As ye would that men should do to you, do ye also to them likewise." (Luke 6:31). It helps if we learn empathy, the ability to see ourselves in the other person's shoes. Pick the phrase in the second column that completes the shoe- or feet-related sentence in the first column.

1. In the Upper Room, Jesus washed the feet of...

a. Moses

2. "I'm not worthy to carry His sandals," said...

b. Ruth

3. "You're standing on holy ground," said God to...

c. Proverbs

4. Those who hastily ate the first Passover, with coat and shoes on were the...

d. a certain woman who led a sinful life

5. A man would give his shoe to another to confirm a decision, according to the book of...

e. His disciples

6. "She washed My feet with her tears and dried them with her hair," said Jesus of...

f. Israelites

7. If we walk the path of life with integrity, we will walk securely, according to the book of...

g. God's Word

8. It's like a lamp to our feet, says the Psalmist of...

h. John the Baptist

PAGE 6/7

```
H E A R D M O R E D O N
Q U N A E B I R K S N I
N L A Z A R U S N A O M
N E A R F A N E C C L E
S H E P H I C A L M E D
N O L B O S Y E W C R O
T H E A L E D M A J O B
A N P L C D E A L O N A
E Y E S R A S E K W O W
T H R A O L A M E A B A
C O S W W E H U D Y E T
O N F E D A N T W I N E
T H E S P O K E C O O R
```

PAGE 8

1. F   2. T (Isaiah 40:15)   3. F
4. T (Proverbs 16:18)
5. F   6. F   7. F   8. T (Job
19:20)   9. F   10. F   11. F
12. T (Ecclesiastes 10:20)

PAGE 9

```
U Y H N V E R E D E E M E R I J
N Y V W S C O B H O Y F E Y D D
H F E S H O Z A O M L K I H U R
Y K T R C E I W Q A L O M O E O
H E I T G S T H E L I F E L A W
C S N S F D S A M W E A Y G E
T O R E G Y H N I I A E L O E H
D L M B R O Y F E G H S X N T
E R F F G N F R O H T U A E O K
V R P K O M A K G T U B H Y D S
O E O S X R O L I Y D P F M N O
L E N T G T T N F N Y B I M A N
E R V E A U Y E T A G F M N A O
B V W O M E K L R L T S V N H F
Y G T F R D R E H P E H S H P G
R V E D U N T C R V R D E S L O
N C A R P E N T E R P O M R A D
```

PAGE 10

1. Kings
2. Disciples
3. Prophets
4. Noah's sons
5. Siblings
6. Priests
7. Family Members
8. Fishermen
9. Missionaries

PAGE 11

```
B E A P L A I N E E D S
R A N A L M O N D X O Y
A C U L A M L C R E N C
M H C M P E I A O M O A
B R O O M T V B A P L M
L U A P P L E E C L I O
E R M I E M A O A F I R
M T I S X F L M C I V E
E A O I I N F E I G E A
V M M C E D A R A D D M
```

166

PAGE 12

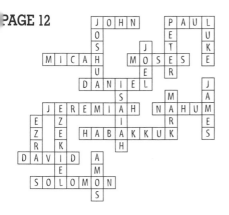

PAGE 13

1. (c) Korah (Numbers 16:1) 2. (a) Saul (1 Samuel 19:10)
3. (b) Ahaz (2 Chronicles 28:1-3) 4.(d) Haman (Esther 3-7)
5. (b) Herod (Matthew 14:1-11)
6. (b) Judas Iscariot (John 6:70-71)

PAGE 14/15

1) Arm is moved in second pew. 2) Lady's earring is missing. 3) Man has glasses on. 4) Pastor's arm is moved. 5) Right flower pot has an extra flower.

PAGE 16

will, news, night, good

PAGE 18

1. b 2. c 3. b 4. a
5. a 6. c 7. c 8. a
9. c 10. a 11. b 12. a

PAGE 17

1. C (1 Samuel 1)
2. G (Genesis 18)
3. A (2 Corinthians 12)
4. D (Exodus 14)
5. I (Psalm 51)
6. H (Matthew 8)
7. E (1 Kings 3)
8. B (Luke 8)
9. F (Luke 15)

ANSWERS

PAGE 19

```
T R O P L M N U Y H T A R F E D
S T F B R D E W S X A L A A B N
S T U T J P T B O P L M M U Y N Y
U B N F M E L M E P I S T L E P
D U E I A N N T B R C E W E Q S
Y L M B N C E T G S D I Y T T M
O Y U V N W Q F A M E N Y T V O
F G R W A B U B E T B T R E Y N
E O T W S X B O I R E E M R E
N L S C D A W M I Y T U T B O Y
D O N I T Y T B R I V A C P D T
T T I A L H I L P O M N I O S H O
I A L L E R B M I T F E O R G T
M H A D U J N O L I M P G O I E
E C C H B T C V E O D B O N K P
S S I N H U J P A R A B L E D O
B E S C F D A Y O F R E S T O
H B U T G O T W R E D K I M A R
L K M H G F O S S Q W E O T L
E C R D T Y H D I T M O L L Y K
F I R S T F I V E B O O K S L D
V R F B G T M U J Y N R G B O K
O L P K I I D O L B U B Y Y H
```

PAGE 20

```
Y G T S I T P A B E H T N H O J
R V E D U N T C R V R D E H M I
N T F E L T G H J L J Q A U I O
U Y J N U E X W D Y N O L M I J
N J O N A H D C U K N H S G Y N
H F B S P X Z P O M L K I H U N
Y B T V C E S W O A L O M I U H
H B Y T S A M S O N L C I M O A
L J J H G F E S A E W E R T V J
E C E D T S H N U J M O L M I I L
P L O S G T Y M E C W S X C E
V L F B U M A H A R B A G R I L
O U P K I S Y N G B U B E Y V R
D A V I D A D F A K E T F M I P
F S N U G T D A N I E L I M O L
Y R V E O U Y N T P A F M N V C
D V W O M I K L P L T G V N B H
```

PAGE 21

1. Belief, 2. Walk In Faith
3. Passover Lamb
4. Narrow Gate

PAGE 22

1. God places... 2. Noah builds... 3. Abraham... 4. Joseph .... 5. Ten Commandments... 6. King David... 7. Solomon's... 8. Gabriel... 9. John the Baptist... 10. Jesus is baptized... 11. Jesus teaches... 12. Jesus dies... 13. Paul spreads... 14. The Apostle John...

PAGE 23

simon, james or phillip, matthew, peter, andrew, john

PAGE 24

In all thy ways acknowled him, and he shall direct th paths. Proverbs 3:6

PAGE 25

1 - D, 2 - G, 3 - A, 4 - F, 5 -
6 - C, 7 - E — 1 - C, 2 - G,
3 - A, 4 - F, 5 - D, 6 - B, 7 -

PAGE 26/27

b, 2. a, 3. b, 4. b, 5. c, 6. a, 7. c, 8. b, 9. a, 10. b, 11. c, 12. b

PAGE 28

, I am with you always. Matthew 28:20

PAGE 29

- Messiah, 2 - Nazarene, 3 - Redeemer, 4 - Mediator,
- Counselor, 6 - Alpha, 7 - Emmanuel

PAGE 30

a (Genesis 3:15) 2. c (Luke 2:36-38) 3. c (Acts 9:40)
b (Genesis 30:21) 5. b (Ruth 1:15-17) 6. a (2 Kings 22:14)
c (Mark 16:9)

PAGE 31

b (Genesis 26:5),
a (1 Samuel 7:12).
c (John 1:41),
a (John 9:7),
c (Exodus 20:10-11),
b (John 14:26),
c (Titus 3:7),
b (Colossians 4:16)

PAGE 32/33

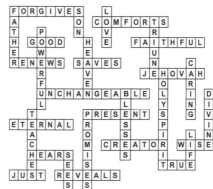

PAGE 34/35

1) Lady in the background is moved. 2) Little boy is looking the other way. 3) Sign is lower. 4) Woman in the middle is wearing an earring. 5) Lady's dress is longer.

PAGE 36

1. ARK (GENESIS 7:1)   2. COLT (MARK 11:7)
3. CHARIOT (ACTS 8:28-31)   4. BOAT (MATTHEW 14:29)
5. FISH (JONAH 1:17)   6. LADDER (GENESIS 28:12)
7. CAMEL (GENESIS 24:61)   8. HORSE (REVELATION 6:2)

PAGE 37

B. Abel, Noah, Jacob, Matthew, Paul   C. Lot, Amos, King Herod, Jesus, Timothy   D. Joshua, David, Solomon, Micah, Luke

PAGE 38

```
E C Z E P H A N I A H O L M I K
P L O B G T Y H A C I M X C E D
V R L B G T M U J Y N T G B H K
O J E R E M I A H E U B H Y I R
P O I S X A D F Z K L P F M S P
F E N U G T W E O U Y I I M A L
Y L A M O S K N T H A F J N I C
D V D O M I K L P A R G O A A H
U Y H N E E X M D B N N N M H J
N Y V L S I A G G A H H A G Y N
S A M U E L Z P O K L K H H U N
Y B T V A E S W Q K L O M I U U
H B Y C G V T F R U D C I M O M
L K H H G F D S A K W E R T V R
Y I T F R D O B A D I A H H I Y
R V H O S E A C R V R D E S M I
N T F E Y T G H J L P O M U I O
```

PAGE 39

1. a 2. a 3. b 4. c
5. b 6. b 7. c

PAGE 40

(Answers will vary)

```
        I
       A S P
     S T R U M
   M A C A D A M
 S T O N E W A L L
U N W I L L I N G L
```

```
H A P P Y Z O O F (S I M E O N)
P I D R O E N L A I S R S P E
E M (R E U B E N) N S A O T I L
S Y U T W U R Y D S A M H E L
O L E V E L I L T A S H E R I
(J U D A H) U L E O M N A R U E
U L E L I N E V A L I N T G O
D L N E D T M (I S S A C H A R)
Y A Y I M Y S O Z Z R A E D Y
O S N A P H T A L I) S L L E A
P A U L N I A N H O J E L L E
H M N E Z N N (N I M A J N E B)
```

PAGE 42/43

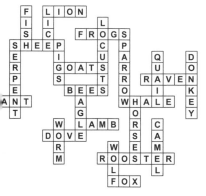

PAGE 44

1. JERICHO
2. BABEL
3. NAZARETH
4. TARSUS
5. PERGA
6. MOAB
7. EMMAUS
8. JERUSALEM
9. NINEVEH
10. ENOCH

PAGE 45

1. b (Matthew 13:31)
2. d (Ruth 2:23)
3. a (John 1:48)
4. d (Matthew 3:4)
5. a (Luke 22:17, 19)
6. b (Matthew 14:17)

PAGE 46/47

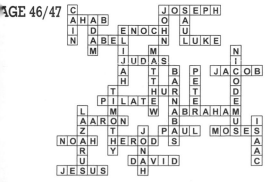

PAGE 48

Judges, Ruth, Acts, Numbers, Mark, Lamentations, James, Revelation, Job, Kings, Psalms, Proverbs, Luke, Esther

PAGE 49

1) Cornelius (Acts 10:1) 2) Zephaniah (Zephaniah 1:1)
3) Alexander (2 Timothy 4:14) 4) Methuselah (Genesis 5:25)
5) Bathsheba (2 Samuel 11:3) 6) Bartimaeus (Mark 10:46)
7) Ahasuerus (Esther 1:1) 8) Elimelech (Ruth 1:2)

PAGE 50

I can do all things through Christ which strengtheneth me.
Philippians 4:13

PAGE 51

God is love. 1 John 4:16

PAGE 52/53

1) Arches are lower.
2) Pastor's nose is smaller. 3) Book is larger. 4) Bride's dress is smaller. 5) Woman in the front pew has hand moved.

PAGE 54/55

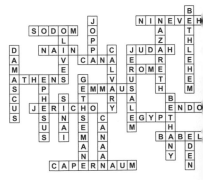

PAGE 56

1 - e (John 6:5-13),

2 - g (1 Kings 3:16-28),

3 - a (Mark 5:35-42),

4 - f (Acts 12:13),

5 - b (Exodus 2:10),

6 - i (Luke 2:46-47),

7 - c (John 4:46-53),

8 - d (1 Samuel 1:24-28),

9 - h (Genesis 21:3)

PAGE 57

```
O L H A N N A H G B U B H Y V R
P E W S X A D F H N A O M I F A
F R U T H T W N U U Y B I M Q L
E V E A A U Y N L X R A C H E L
D V N O P I K L D T T G V N L I
Y I T M R D E S A A Q A E E I C
D V E A O N T B H T R L E S Z S
N T E R Y T I H J L A O M T A I
U Y C T V T X A D D N M M H B R
N A V H H E H R G E O H A E E P
S N E A Q T Z A G B L K I R T N
Y N T V I E M S O O L O R I H U
H A Y T G Y T H R R M C I M O M
L O J H R E A N N A W E M T V A
E J R A T E H N I H M O R M I R
P L M B L T R E B E K A H C E Y
V R J U D I T H J Y N T G B I K
```

PAGE 58

1. c. Naomi (in-law) 2. a. Mary (sister) 3. b. Onesimus (master) 4. d. Abraham (grandson) 5. b. Miriam (brother) 6. c. Michal (husband) 7. a. Isaac (wife)

PAGE 59

Deborah	d. Judge (Judges 4:4)
Paul	f. Tentmaker (Acts 18:3)
Baruch	h. Scribe (Jeremiah 36:4)
Luke	i. Physician (Colossians 4:14)
Zacchaeus	b. Tax Collector (Luke 19:2)
Lydia	g. Merchant (Acts 16:14)
Andrew	c. Fisher (Matthew 4:18)
Amos	a. Shepherd (Amos 1:1)
Dorcas	e. Tailor (Acts 9:39)

PAGE 60

Samuel

ANSWERS

PAGE 61 (Answers will vary)

1. tent   2. Abba   3. dead   4. Miriam   5. Nain
6. David   7. Eagle   8. acacia   9. widow
10. ruler   11. deed   12. river

PAGE 62/63

PAGE 64/65

1) Lampshade is larger. 2) Arm on chair is different. 3) Young girl's eyebrows are missing. 4) Young girls pants are longer. 5) Table has moved closer

PAGE 66

1. (a)   2. (c)   3. (a)   4. (b)   5. (c)   6. (a)

PAGE 67

Andrew

PAGE 68/69

1) Church has one less window. 2) Stop sign is shorter. 3) Car grill is different. 4) Girl's pony tail is gone. 5) Mirror is gone.

PAGE 70

Ask and ye shall receive that your joy may be full.
John 16:24

PAGE 71

1. Jacob's Ladder, 2. Do Everything with Love
3. Trust In Him, 4. Rainbow

PAGE 72

Speak; for thy servant heareth. 1 Samuel 3:10

PAGE 73

bushel, barley, cubits, Red Sea, donkey, church, Sunday

PAGE 74/75

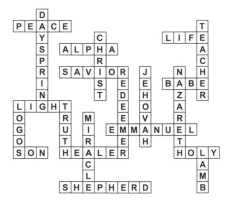

PAGE 76

Haggai, Philemon, Galatians, Obadiah, Ecclesiastes,
Hebrews, Philippians, Habakkuk, Nahum, Psalms,
Timothy, Colossians

ANSWERS

PAGE 77

```
O O W L S O M E U M E L O O K S A W
I S E E K S A A R O N E N S U I G E
B R E E A S T C A O R N B E A D R S
C E P J T O T C L H A G G A I I E S
A A S P E N H E E D B E O O D E E D
V R A Y M T E Q U E S M P O R T D O
R A C L A I W R E S S O M M D R I M
E C C L E S I A S T E S E E T T L E
J E U V E A X T C O L O S S I A N S
S U S S E A I A R R N O T R P R I H
E T E R C C O H A B A K K U K E O E
S T R O O P B E E R S H E B A A N E
R E S U F F E R I C C A E P R M I P
P L U G G E P H I L I P P I A N S O
A I L A A G E W C O Z Z I L L E E D
F U L F I L L M E N T E P L L E E V
I U A F H E L E W E O D P A O T L O
```

PAGE 78/79

1) Bricks by window are missing.
2) Lady's leg has moved. 3) Hat has a band on it.
4) Steps have moved.
5) Tree has moved.

PAGE 80/81

```
E N I W F L A M B
L S E V I L O E D
T A T H S E S R M
L E N G H I A F I
E R M I N T T S L
E U T O X U B S K
K E B U B E A N S
S E M E N B R Y E
L G E S U T L A S
S G I E T A E H W
D S A F S M Y E N
C O R N Y E N O H
```

Let these gifts to us be blessed. Amen

PAGE 82/83

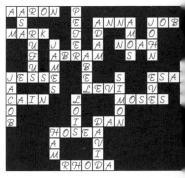

PAGE 84/85

1) Robe is shorter. 2) Manger has moved down. 3) Brick on the right is missing. 4) Windows on dome are different. 5) Star is smaller.

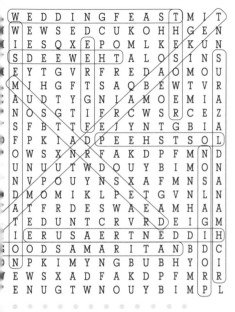

The eyes of the LORD are upon the righteous, and his ears are open unto their cry.
Psalm 34:15

ANSWERS

177

PAGE 89

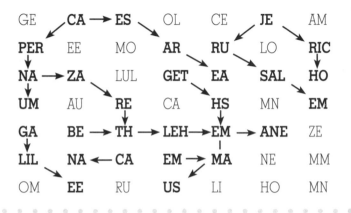

PAGE 90/91

BIBLE PLACES: 1 - B, 2 - G, 3 - A, 4 - H, 5 - I, 6 - D, 7 - E, 8 - F, 9 - C
BIBLE PEOPLE: 1-G, 2 - E, 3 - I, 4 - H, 5 - A, 6 - D, 7 - C, 8 - B, 9 - F

PAGE 92/93

1) Boy in front row has a different tie. 2) Boy in back row eyes closed. 3) Girl's hand in back row has moved. 4) Choir teacher arm has moved. 5) Bands on sleeve are missing.

PAGE 94

1. star / rats, 2. dew / wed, 3. keep / peek, 4. ten / net,
5. bard / drab, 6. rood / door, 7. step / pets, 8. war / raw,
9. nib / bin, 10. loop / pool, 11. sleep / peels, 12. pal / lap,
13. mad / dam, 14. tops / spot

PAGE 95 (Answers will vary. Here's our list:)

true, sate, gate, soak, soon, moon, tame, neat, rage, meat,
soar, rare, tare, gear, sane, sage, none, tram

PAGE 96/97

1. HEAVENS, MOON, STARS
2. EARTH
3. TREE, RIVERS
4. MOON, SUN
5. HEAVEN, EARTH, SEAS
6. EARTH, MOUNTAINS, SEA
7. EARTH, HILLS
8. CLOUDS, SKIES
9. FIELD, TREES, WOOD

PAGE 98

1. Fine
2. Rest
3. Address
4. Nice
5. Cast
6. Issue
7. Sewer
Saint's Name:
Francis

PAGE 99

```
O L P K I E Y N G B U B H Y V R
P J W S X A M F A K D P F M I P
F E N U G T W M Q T A R S U S L
Y R C A P E R N A U M F M N N C
D U W N M I K L P U A G V N A A
Y S T T R D E P H A S U S H Z P
R A E I U N T C R V C D E S A P
N L F O B T G H J L U O M U R O
U E H C V E X H D E S O L M E J
N M V H S E T C U K R H B G T N
H F E S Q N Z H Q M L I I J H N
Y B T V I E S W L A L O C I N U
H B Y R G V A F T E D C I H O P
L K O H G F N S Y Q H E R T O R
E C R D T Y A E R A S E A C I K
P L O B G T C F E C W S M C E D
V R F B G T M U J Y N T G B I K
```

PAGE 100/101

1. b, 2. a,
3. c, 4. b,
5. c, 6. a,
7. c, 8. c,
9. a, 10. b,
11. b, 12. c,
13. a, 14. b

PAGE 102/103

1. 1 Corinthians 13–the great "love chapter" of Paul's letter to the Corinthians.
2. Cain's response to God when God inquired about his murdered brother.
3. The first words of Psalm 23, the "Shepherd Psalm."
4. Pontius Pilate's words to the crowd as he presented to them Jesus, bleeding.
5. Moses' words to Pharaoh, pleading for the release of the Israelites.
6. The angel Gabriel's words to Mary announcing her role in the birth of Jesus.
7. Ruth's words to her mother-in-law after both women were widowed.
8. Jesus' question to Judas Iscariot.
9. Mordecai's question to Queen Esther as he pleads for her help.
10. Adam's words to Eve in the Garden of Eden.
11. Joseph's words to Potiphar's wife.
12. Jesus' commandment to Peter after Jesus' resurrection.

PAGE 104

Let us hold fast the profession of our faith without wavering; for he is faithful that promised.
Hebrews 10:23

PAGE 105

1. The Israelites celebrate...   2. After 430 years in Egypt...

3. The Israelites cross the Red Sea...   4. God sends manna...

5. Moses receives the Ten Commandments from God...

6. Aaron makes a golden calf...   7. Out of anger,...

8. Moses receives the Commandments a second time...

9. The Israelites build... 10. Moses dies...   11. Joshua sends spies...

12. Joshua leads the Israelites...

PAGE 106

```
T O S N A P D R A G O N I N G
B E A M S Z D A F F O D I L I
U M Z S E N E S L I L U R S N
T E A U T I V A I N E D R A G
T N L M O E Q I V I O L E T S
A R E C Q U R L P O R D S I S
O C A R N A T I O N H A I A W
N P W I T I N G S I R I S E E
P E T L L I L Y E M I S P I E
A T U M I N S P A N S Y E U T
Z U L I A L U M S O E S O N P
I N I A S O A L I R I N N S E
R I P E N S Y C P O P P Y P A
M A R I G O L D C S I C O R I
U C Z I N N I A M E N O S I S
M A M S S T E N N O B E U L B
```

PAGE 107

1 - e,

2 - g,

3 - a,

4 - i,

5 - j,

6 - b,

7 - h,

8 - c,

9 - f,

10 - d

PAGE 108

1. Continue in...Colossians 4:2   2. Trust...Proverbs 3:5

3. Come...Matthew 11:28   4. A wise...Proverbs 1:5

5. Wait...Psalm 27:14   6. I am...John 6:35

7. The Lord...Numbers 6:24

PAGE 109

1 - Nathanael, Peter, Andrew; 2 - Melchizedek, Eli, Samuel;
3 - Judah, Gilgal, Galilee; 4 - Genesis, Judges, Psalms;
5 - Corinthians, Romans, Galatians; 6 - Ruth, Esther, Rebekah;
7 - John, Matthew, Luke; 8 - Elizabeth, Mary, Leah; 9 - Ahab,
David, Herod; 10 - Elijah, Amos, Ezekiel; 11 - Naomi, Orpah,
Anna; 12 - Paul, Daniel, Joseph

PAGE 110/111

Parable: Prodigal Son, Loyal Father

PAGE 112/113

PAGE 114

Answers: (Yours may vary.) beak, back, cask, clad, clam, cram,
dais, dame, dead, dear, dock, lack, lame, mask, orca, rack, road,
roam, roar, rock, rode, same

PAGE 115

1 - b, 2 - a, 3 - d, 4 - c, 5 - a, 6 - c, 7 - b, 8 - a

PAGE 116

1. b 2. a 3. b 4. a 5. c 6. c 7. b 8. a 9. b 10. c

PAGE 117

1. b (Genesis 30:20-21), 2. a (2 Samuel 12:24),
3. c (Numbers 26:59), 4. b (Matthew 1:5), 5. a (Genesis 4:25),
6. b (1 Samuel 1:20), 7. b (2 Timothy 1:5), 8. c (Mark 16:1),
9. a (Matthew 1:16)

PAGE 118

1. c (Genesis 4:9), 2. a (Matthew 22:39), 3. b (John 19:5),
4. a (Luke 1:38) 5. c (Matthew 5:1-9), 6. b (Acts 3:6),
7. c (Esther 4:15-16)

PAGE 119

Samuel, Corinthians, Timothy, Obadiah, Chronicles, Joshua,
Proverbs, Philemon, Haggai, Galatians, Hebrews, Esther,
Zechariah

PAGE 120/121

A - Peter (Mark 14:72),
B - Sarah (Genesis 17:17;
18:10), C - Simeon and Anna
(Luke 2:25-38), D - David
(1 Samuel 17:49), E - Paul
(Acts 9:1-6), F - Noah (Genesis
7:1), G - Ruth (Ruth 4:13),
H - Martha (Luke 10:41-42)

PAGE 122/123

PAGE 124/125

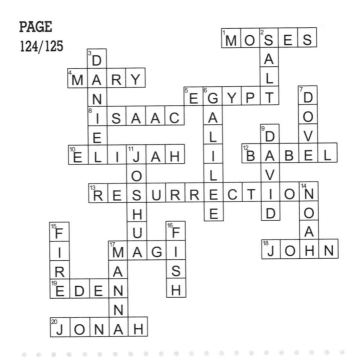

PAGE 126/127

```
W Z C K (K N O C K) S F (D R A E H)
J E P R A S Y Z I J O D Q U P N
L (D U N D N J Y N G L U Q F X Z
I  J E K V Y B Y Z L Q J G R K X
T K T L T W H K W E O C P H W O
P K R D E S K T O S X R I T C
M L R R M V A M J S H Q I R A D
Y D A E W W E R L A R I Y L S N
T H C R Q O T R U Z X A L A A S
L E G H F W U O E W D U E L A K
J (O P E N E D) M H D P C L F L K
I X X J E U X Z S O E E Q N Y F
Y K P X P U H U N C T F S N N M
Q E A C W R U N I Y X V V J R H
T T S G U D H L P Q R (K E E S) N
S B V O T W R Y P S A E N O J O
J E N Y Y O M K K S R R W U A U
E O M R Z A W F W B E T J S P Q
H U E M Q J Z Q Q W P J N M N T
J D T B N R B R K K U M I J P A
```

Possible solutions:

1. HURT	2. FEAR	4. REAL	5. TRUE
hart	tear	teal	tree
halt	team	tell	free
hale	tram	till	fret
bale	pram	tile	feet
balm	PRAY	rile	fest
CALM		rife	lest
	3. STAY	LIFE	lost
	slay		lose
	flay		LOVE
	fray		
	frat		
	fret		
	FREE		

Saying: Two things are bad for the heart—running upstairs and running down people.

ANSWERS

PAGE 130/131

PAGE 132/133

D	E	E	R			R	A	G	S
O	P	T	I	C		U	T	A	H
T	E	N	O	R		N	A	M	E
S	E	A		E	D		L	E	D
			R	A	I	S	E	S	
	G	U	I	T	A	R			
P	A	L		E	L		C	A	P
O	U	T	S		O	P	I	N	E
E	Z	R	A		G	H	A	N	A
M	E	A	N			D	O	E	S

Possible
Solutions:

3. LESS
loss
lose
lore
MORE

1. TINY
ine
vine
vane
vase
VAST

4. MEAN
mead
mend
mind
KIND

2. POOR
pool
poll
pole
pile
ile
ice
RICH

5. HOLD
hole
pole
pale
pave
gave
GIVE

1. D (1 Samuel 17)
2. H (Genesis 12)
3. A (Judges 4)
4. F (2 Corinthians 6)
5. I (Acts 9)
6. J (Esther 4)
7. B (Exodus 3)
8. G (Matthew 1)
9. C (Mark 1)
10. E (Jonah 1)

PAGE 136/137

Answers: dermis, glower, tulip, caravan, hobnob, yolk

I have been driven many times to my knees by the overwhelming conviction that I had absolutely no other place to go.

1. Eve's sheaves
2. Luke's dukes
3. Noah's boas
4. Ruth's booths
5. Aaron's herons
6. Mark's parks
7. Paul's stalls
8. John's fawns

1. J	7. D
2. K	8. I
3. A	9. E
4. F	10. C
5. H	11. G
6. B	

ANSWERS

PAGE 144

1. A 2. C 3. B 4. C 5. B 6. A 7. B 8. C 9. B 10. A

* *

PAGE 145

1. CARNATION 2. DAFFODIL 3. GLADIOLUS
4. SNAPDRAGON 5. PANSY 6. AZALEA
7. DAHLIA   Answer: DAISIES

* *

PAGE 146/147

* *

PAGE 148

Answers: head, hold, box, strong

PAGE 149

1. B
2. A
3. B
4. C
5. A
6. A
7. C
8. A
9. B
10. B

PAGE 150/151

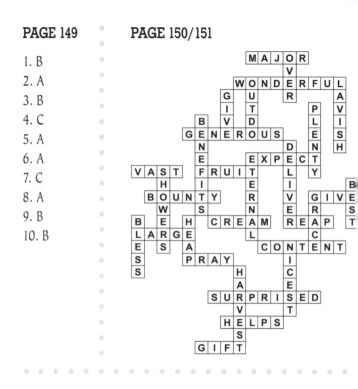

PAGE 152

S	1. sheets	2. these	3. thee	S
U	4. mouse	5. some	6. ose	M
N	7. sprain	8. pairs	9. spar	I
N	10. lemon	11. mole	12. Moe	L
Y	13. teary	14. rate	15. tar	E

PAGE 153

1. Fine 2. Sole 3. Well 4. Fair 5. Bow 6. Lead 7. Ground
8. Tip 9. Desert 10. Wind 11. Rose

PAGE 154/155

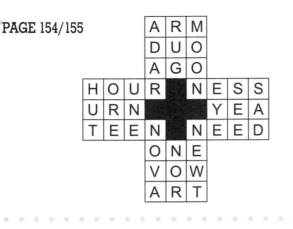

			A	R	M			
			D	U	O			
			A	G	O			
H	O	U	R	■	N	E	S	S
U	R	N	■	■	■	Y	E	A
T	E	E	N	■	N	E	E	D
			O	N	E			
			V	O	W			
			A	R	T			

PAGE 156

1. F (Matthew 14:24-25) 2. H (Luke 23:44-46) 3. B (Genesis 7:12)
4. A (Acts 2:2-4) 5. C (Exodus 10:13-20) 6. D (1 Kings 19:11-12)
7. G (Matthew 28:2-6) 8. E (Jonah 4:6-8)

PAGE 157

1. C
2. A
3. B
4. A
5. C
6. A
7. B
8. B

PAGE 158/159

```
H Y D R A N G E A P O Y G
N J Z M U I N I H P L E D
Z N H Y A C I N T H L D M
Q P P Y L O O Y Y J C A F
A I B E S O R N E D R A G
C L X A E H E U J I X Y D
N U X U J A M R G J C A Y
Y T D A I S Y O F Z F N S
R S I R I B L Y F F V W S
O S A F P D U S O D E T X
L X V X A Q A D X E D H U
G A P U M M I T W E A E
G S A D A L U P S E W K T
N U N A R R E I S E D X E
I C S H Y A Y O N I E G F
N O Y L L R R P H A A R E
R R N I L M I C P B R R F
O C O A I C R K V O P E E
M B E R S O T Z X M P L G
E A P J I L L E B E U L B
```

191

PAGE 160

1. Think clearly
2. Research
3. Objectivity
4. Discernment
5. Root cause
6. Planning
Answer:
PRAYER

PAGE 164

Answer: watch,
coffee, pace,
Maker

PAGE 165

1. E
2. H
3. A
4. F
5. B
6. D
7. C
8. G

PAGE 161

1. G   2. A   3. I   4. C   5. H
6. E   7. B   8. F   9. D

PAGE 162/163

The heart of the
prudent getteth
knowledge;
and the ear of
the wise seeketh
knowledge.

Proverbs 18:15